chess
endings

chess
endings
essential knowledge

by Yuri Averbakh

EVERYMAN CHESS

First published in 1993 by Gloucester Publishers plc, (formerly Everyman Publishers plc), Northburgh House, 10 Northburgh Street, London, EC1V 0AT

Copyright © 1993 Gloucester Publishers plc

First edition 1996
Reprinted 1971, 1973 (twice), 1976, 1978, 1982, 1986
Second edition 1987
Third edition 1993
Reprinted 1997, 1999

British Library Cataloguing-in-Publication Data
A catalogue record for this book is available from the British Library.

ISBN 1 85744 022 6

Distributed in North America by The Globe Pequot Press, P.O Box 480, 246 Goose Lane, Guilford, CT 06437-0480.

All other sales enquiries should be directed to Gloucester Publishers plc, Northburgh House, 10 Northburgh Street, London, EC1V 0AT
tel: 020 7253 7887 fax: 020 7490 3708
email: info@everymanchess.com
website: www.everymanchess.com

Everyman is the registered trade mark of Random House Inc. and is used in this work under license from Random House Inc.

Printed and bound in the UK

Contents

Translator's Foreword

The endgame can be a hard and in some respects disturbing school for the vast majority of chess players. Any deficiencies in positional judgement or technique which may have remained unnoticed amidst the complexities of the opening and middlegame are here ruthlessly revealed; errors stand out in greater relief and, what is worse, generally have more serious consequences; while theoretical knowledge now becomes not only desirable but even an indispensable item of the player's equipment. Paradoxically, therefore, the very simplicity of the endgame adds in practice to its difficulty and lends it, in the minds of many, an air of mystery.

From a player's approach to and treatment of this final phase of the struggle one can obtain a reliable indication of his or her true strength and ability. The hand of the master is readily distinguishable, and it is no accident that most of the world champions, from Steinitz to the latest title-holder, are looked upon as virtuosi of the endgame. In the USSR, where the study of chess has been raised to scientific levels, the need to perfect technical skill in endings as well as the earlier parts of the game has been appreciated for a long time, and the author of this book has probably done more than anyone else to further this. Grandmaster Yuri Averbakh is the Soviet Union's leading expert on endgame theory and headed the team that produced the multi-volume *Shakhmatnye Okonchaniya* (*Chess Endings*), which enjoys a worldwide reputation in this field.

The present book, designed on less comprehensive lines, contains all the basic material necessary to take a player from the stage of beginner to that of regular tournament competitor. The subjects covered include the elementary mates, the pieces in combat (both against each other and against pawns) and pawn promotion, while the last chapter is devoted to practical endings – examples, that is, from real games.

If you read this book conscientiously, you will benefit not merely from an improvement in your play in the endgame itself but on a much

1

broader plane. In the first place, Averbakh's clear and logical explanations will develop your understanding of the mechanics of the chessboard and the forces deployed on it. Secondly, your conduct of the middlegame will gain in assurance, since it must always be borne in mind that an objective decision may at any moment depend upon knowing a simple type of ending. With the information given in these chapters at your command you should never find yourself positively avoiding the transition to the endgame, and to that extent you will be a more complete player.

Peter H. Clarke
Morwenstow, Cornwall

From the Author

The concluding phase of the game is the Achilles' heel of the majority of chess enthusiasts. How many times have I observed in a simultaneous display how some player has understood the opening quite well, and has conducted the middlegame quite tolerably, but after the exchange of a number of pieces he has begun to 'drift', and as a result has lost an elementary ending.

I conceived the idea of writing a popular booklet devoted to the endgame back in the early 1950s, when I was working on an encyclopaedic reference work intended for players of high standard. Out of the mass of information on the endgame, I thought it was important to select the minimum which any chess enthusiast should know in order to handle competently the concluding phase of the game. It turned out that it was not necessary to know such a great deal.

The first Russian edition of this work was published in 1960. The small booklet was warmly received by average chess enthusiasts, and it was translated into ten languages.

Since then a quarter of a century has passed . When it was suggested to me that a new edition of this booklet should be published, I at first wanted to write something new, and to expand it to take account of the achievements of modern theory. But on reflection I realised that the main virtue of this booklet is in fact that it is not overloaded with material, and that it gives only the most essential information, that which a chess enthusiast really needs. Anyone who wishes to know more can be referred to more voluminous reference works. But in this booklet I have decided to leave everything as it is, restricting myself only to corrections and additions which are absolutely necessary.

Yuri Averbakh

Introduction

In the course of the struggle that takes place on the chessboard the forces on both sides are gradually expended, the position becomes simplified, and the play passes into the final, decisive phase – the endgame. At this stage the player is usually confronted by one of three tasks: to exploit the advantage he has gained in the earlier part of the game and convert it into a win; or neutralise his opponent's advantage by accurate defence and draw the game; or finally, having failed to gain an advantage in the middlegame, he can try to obtain it here.

The endgame begins when there is a relatively small number of pieces left on the board and, but for the rare exception, direct attacks on the king with the combinational complications typical of the middlegame are impossible. The concluding stage of a game of chess has its characteristic peculiarities which, in comparison with the middlegame, alter the whole appoach to the position and the significance of the forces in action on the board.

The first important feature distinguishing the endgame from the other stages of the game is that the king takes an active part in the play. Having 'sat out' the whole game behind the pawn bastions in its own camp, the king now becomes an active, attacking piece and tries to participate in the struggle with all its might. It falls upon the opponent's pieces and pawns and is often the first to force its way into the enemy camp.

Comparatively few pieces are left on the board in the endgame, but their relative value is considerably increased. For success it is important to know how to get the the maximum activity out of the pieces and to organise the co-operation of the pieces among themselves and with the pawns. To play the endgame correctly means to make one's fighting forces active to the greatest possible extent and to assure their smooth co-operation.

In the endgame it is rarely possible, even with a big material advantage, to mate the opponent's king at once: one lacks the force to do it. In order to obtain a sufficient material superiority one must promote one or several pawns. This means that since every 'insignificant' pawn may, given the chance, become a mighty piece – a queen – its role here is greatly increased. Pawn promotion is one of the strategic tasks of the endgame.

It is relatively easier to study the endgame with its small number of pieces and pawns than it is the other stages of the game. In the development of chess theory over the last 100 years dozens of endgame positions have been thoroughly analysed and published in the literature of the game. In these positions the best methods of attack and defence have been found and the final outcome, granted correct play on both sides, has been determined. Furthermore, for many endings typical playing procedures have been established and auxiliary methods worked out which permit a rapid and accurate appreciation of the position. Endings which have been investigated like this are called theoretical. In playing these endings, which are often far from easy, accurate knowledge is of the first importance; when it is put to proper use, the game inevitably ends in its preordained result.

Play does not become theoretical immediately the endgame is reached, though even in the most complicated positions typical manoeuvres have now been elaborated and the best ways of playing discovered. Normally, the problem in a complex ending is to transpose into the sort of positions that have already been studied.

When learning chess one ought to begin with an analysis of simple positions with a small number of fighting units. And these, as a rule, are endgame positions. By analysing straightforward endings with the most varied combinations of material the beginner can get to know the special characteristics of the various pieces and the mechanism of their struggle against each other. Having acquired a 'feel' for the properties of the different pieces, he may the more easily understand the way they work together. Thus, the study of the simplest endings should precede the analysis of the openings and the middlegame.

The author has made it his task to provide the reader with the essential minimum knowledge of the endgame, to acquaint him with the basic theoretical positions, and finally to teach him the most important strategic motifs and the simplest ways of making a quick assessment of the position.

The Properties of the Pieces

In the endgame the strength of each piece stands out in greater relief than in the other stages of the game. For this reason it is useful to recall what we know about the properties of the pieces.

The knight. Not a long-range piece, it attacks squares that are comparatively near to it. Eight squares come under simultaneous fire from the knight when it is stationed in the centre of the board, but as it approaches the edge the number it can attack at the same time diminishes – or, as it is commonly put, its striking power decreases. In the corner of the board the knight can attack only two squares; in other words, its striking power goes down fourfold. It is clear that centralisation enables the knight to display its strength to the full. The knight differs from all the other pieces in its right to jump over pieces and pawns. Because of this its powers do not diminish in closed positions.

The following property of the knight is interesting: if it stands, for example, on a black square, it can attack another black square only in an uneven number of moves and a white square only in an even number.

The bishop. This is a long-range piece. Its striking power alters from thirteen squares when it is in the centre to seven at the edge of the board. Centralisation enhances the bishop's possibilities. Thanks to its long-range action it is better than the knight at handling play on two flanks. If its sphere of action is restricted by pawns, its strength decreases. The bishop needs clear diagonals.

The rook. A long-range piece, it attacks exactly fourteen squares from any point on the board. Its striking power, therefore, does not depend on its placing. To display its strength to the best the rook needs space – open lines (ranks and files).

The queen. This is the piece with the greatest range. The striking power of the queen alters from twenty-seven squares when it is in the centre to twenty-one at the edge of the board. Centralisation heightens its fighting qualities. To display its powers fully the queen also needs open space (ranks, files, and diagonals).

That, briefly, is all it is necessary to know about the individual pieces before beginning to study the endgame.

1 Mating the Lone King

Mate with a Queen

The queen cannot give mate unaided; this can only be achieved by the united efforts of the king and queen. Nor can the king be mated in the centre of the board; one must drive it to the edge. The quickest way to do this is by the concerted action of the king and queen.

1

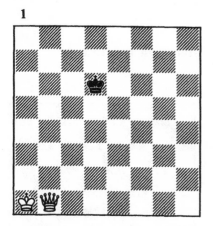

First, we bring the king into play.

1 ♔b2 ♚d5 2 ♔c3 ♚e5 3 ♕g6

The queen comes into the game and severely limits the enemy king's sphere of action.

3 ... ♚f4 4 ♚d4 ♚f3 5 ♕g5 ♚f2 6 ♕g4 ♚e1 7 ♕g2

Now, with the king cut off on the edge of the board, mate is not far away.

7 ... ♚d1 8 ♚d3 ♚c1 9 ♕c2 mate

It does not usually take more than ten moves to force mate in such endings.

7 ♕g2 was not the only move. White could have played 7 ♚e3 ♚f1 8 ♕g6 ♚e1 9 ♕g1 mate.

However, instead of 8 ♕g6, it would be a bad mistake to play 8 ♕g3??, since then the black king would have nowhere to go – it would be a stalemate position and the game would be a draw.

Beginners often make errors like that. Sometimes, therefore, instructors recommend another, simpler method of mating: this consists in driving the king back with the queen alone and only when it has been forced to the edge of the board bringing one's own king to help. For example:

1 ♕f5

The queen is placed a knight's move from the opponent's king.

1 ... ♔c6

Or 1 ... ♔e7 2 ♕g6.

2 ♕e5 ♔b6 3 ♕d5 ♔c7 4 ♕e6 ♔b7 5 ♕d6 ♔c8 6 ♕e7 ♔b8 7 ♔b2 ♔c8 8 ♔b3 ♔b8 9 ♔b4 ♔c8 10 ♔b5 ♔b8 11 ♔b6 ♔c8 12 ♕c7 mate

This method is longer but it excludes the possibility of stalemate.

Mate with a Rook

Here, too, one must first of all drive the black king to the edge of the board. This can only be achieved by the combined operations of the king and rook.

2

1 ♔b2 ♔d4 2 ♔c2 ♔e4 3 ♔c3 ♔e5 4 ♔c4 ♔e4

When the kings stand opposed like this one can check with the rook and drive the enemy king back.

5 ♖e1+ ♔f5 6 ♔d4 ♔f4 7 ♖f1+ ♔g5 8 ♔e4 ♔g6 9 ♔e5 ♔g5

The black king is also confined to the edge of the board after 9 ... ♔g7 10 ♔e6 ♔g8 11 ♔e7 ♔g7 12 ♖g1+.

10 ♖g1+ ♔h4 11 ♔f5 ♔h3 12 ♔f4 ♔h2 13 ♖g3 ♔h1 14 ♔f3 ♔h2 15 ♔f2 ♔h1 16 ♖h3 mate

Not more than sixteen moves are normally required for this mate.

Mate with Two Bishops

3

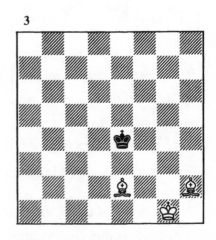

In order to mate with two bishops it is not only necessary to drive the opponent's king to the edge of the board but also into one of the corners. Again, this is accomplished by a combined use of the forces.

1 ♔f2 ♚d4 2 ♗f3 ♚d3 3 ♗e5 ♚d2 4 ♗e4 ♚c1 5 ♚e3!

When driving back a lone king, one must be careful to see that it has free squares to which to retreat. 5 ♚e2?? leads to stalemate and a draw.

5 ... ♚d1 6 ♗b2 ♚e1 7 ♗c2 ♚f1 8 ♚f3 ♚g1

Or 8 ... ♚e1 9 ♗c3+ ♚f1 10 ♗d3+ ♚g1 11 ♚g3 ♚h1 12 ♗d2 ♚g1 13 ♗e3+ ♚h1 14 ♗e4 mate.

9 ♗f5 ♚f1 10 ♗c3 ♚g1 11 ♚g3 ♚f1 12 ♗d3+ ♚g1 13 ♗d4+ ♚h1 14 ♗e4 mate

Mate with Bishop and Knight

The mate with bishop and knight is much more complicated than the previous ones. About thirty-five moves are needed to accomplish it. In as much as the present rules limit the number of moves allowed for mate to fifty, these endings demand precise play.

Here the winning process consists of three stages. First, the king is driven to the edge of the board; then into a corner of the colour controlled by the bishop; and there at last it is mated.

We will start by examining how the mate in the corner is executed.

4

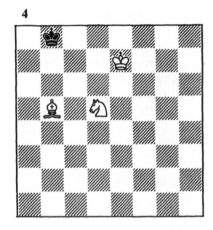

The black king has been driven into the necessary corner and cannot get out. Note the way the pieces co-operate, the one complementing the other. The knight covers the black squares c7 and b6, the bishop the white squares a6 and c6, and the king d8. From here it is mate in not more than nine moves.

For example (with Black to move):

1 ... ♚a7 2 ♚d7 ♚b7 3 ♚d8 ♚b8 4 ♗a6!

Now the king's sphere of movement is still more restricted.

4 ... ♚a7 5 ♗c8 ♚b8 6 ♘b4 ♚a7

7 ♔c7 ♔a8 8 ♗b7+ ♔a7 9 ♘c6
mate

The king can only be mated in a corner of the colour the bishop controls. So, of course, the weaker side strives when retreating to get to one of the other, safe corners. It is therefore very important to know how to drive the enemy king 'across' from one corner to the other.

Here is a typical position.

5

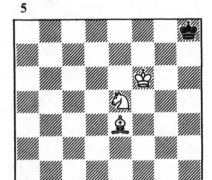

1 ♘f7+ ♔g8 2 ♗f5 ♔f8 3 ♗h7 ♔e8 4 ♘e5 ♔d8!

The most active defence. Black dreams of forcing his way through to the a1 corner. After 4 ... ♔f8 5 ♘d7+ ♔e8 6 ♔e6 ♔d8 7 ♗d3 ♔c7 (7 ... ♔e8 8 ♗b5 ♔d8 9 ♘b6 ♔c7 10 ♘d5+ leads to the same thing) 8 ♗b5 ♔d8 9 ♘b6 ♔c7 10 ♘d5+ ♔d8 11 ♔f7 ♔c8 12 ♔e7 ♔b8 13 ♔d7 White mates in the

manner already considered.

5 ♔e6 ♔c7 6 ♘d7! ♔b7 7 ♗d3!

6 ... ♔c6 would have been answered in the same way.

7 ... ♔c6 8 ♗a6 ♔c7 9 ♗b5 ♔d8 10 ♘b6 ♔c7 11 ♘d5+

White's accurate play has enabled him to cut the black king off and reach a position in which it takes at most nine moves to mate.

This method of driving the king across the board was pointed out by the famous French player, A.Philidor, in 1777.

There is one other position with the king at the edge of the board with which it is useful to be acquainted.

6

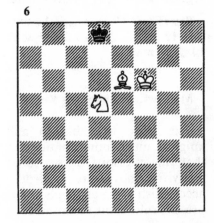

Here the black king tries to "be obstinate".

1 ... ♔e8 2 ♘f4 ♔d8 3 ♔e5!

White need not be afraid of allowing the enemy king some freedom. It is only free temporarily and cannot reach a1.

3 ... ♔c7 4 ♔d5 ♔b6 5 ♗d7!

This is the point: the king is cut off.

5 ... ♔a5 6 ♔c5 ♔a6 7 ♔b4 ♔b6
8 ♘d5+ ♔a6 9 ♗c8+ ♔a7 10 ♔b5

Now the rest is simple, and the reader may like to finish the mate himself for practice.

We shall now consider how to drive the king to the edge of the board.

7

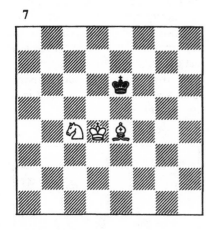

The white force is already mobilised, so it is time to begin the drive.

1 ♗d3 ♔f6 2 ♔d5 ♔f7 3 ♔e5
♔g7 4 ♔e6 ♔f8 5 ♔f6 ♔e8 6 ♘e5
♔f8

After 6 ... ♔d8 7 ♗b5! ♔c7 8 ♘c4! the black king finds itself cut off and confined to the a8 corner.

7 ♗c4 ♔e8 8 ♗f7+ ♔d8

Not 8 ... ♔f8 9 ♘g6 mate.

9 ♔e6! ♔c7 10 ♗e8!

With his last two moves White has allowed the king some scope, but it can no longer escape from the corner.

10 ... ♔b6 11 ♔d6 ♔a5 12 ♔c5

The rest is straightforward, and of this we leave the reader the chance to convince himself.

Had the black king made towards its h1 corner, then White would have shut it in there. For example:

2 ... ♔g5 3 ♔e5 ♔g4 4 ♗c2 ♔h4

4 ... ♔f3 is answered by 5 ♗d1+ blocking the way; while if 4 ... ♔g5 then 5 ♘e3 ♔h6 6 ♔f6 ♔h5 7 ♗g6+ ♔h4 8 ♔f5 ♔g3 9 ♗h5 ♔f2 10 ♔f4 ♔e1 11 ♘c4, and again the king is unable to break through to the safe corner at a1.

5 ♔f5 ♔h5

Or 5 ... ♔g3 6 ♗d1 ♔f2 7 ♔f4.

6 ♘e5 ♔h6 7 ♔f6 ♔h5 8 ♗g6+
♔h4 9 ♔f5 ♔g3 10 ♗h5 ♔f2 11
♔f4 ♔e1 12 ♘c4

And Black's escape is cut off.

It is useful to note that basically it is the king and bishop that drive the opponent's king back. The knight only comes into play occasionally, depriving the king of important squares.

Mate with Two Knights

Against correct defence it is not possible to mate with two knights.

8

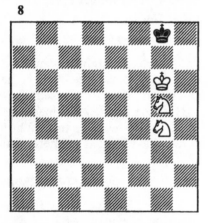

Thus, in this position Black does not answer 1 ♘f6+ with 1 ... ♚h8 because of 2 ♘f7 mate but with **1 ... ♚f8**, moving his king out of the dangerous corner. If White plays 1 ♘e6, preventing the king from getting out, then mate still cannot be forced after **1 ... ♚h8**. In fact, to force mate with the black king on g8 White must be able to check with one knight (from e7, f6, or h6) and then, on ... ♚h8, give the final check with the other from f7. The knight that administers the mate from f7 must control the f8 square and, consequently, it must be on d7, e6, or h7. But White does not have time to transfer this knight to f7 because the black king has no moves and will be stalemated.

It is another matter if Black has a pawn as well. In this case it will be harmful to him – there will be no stalemate, and White will have time to mate.

In some positions where Black has a pawn White wins even if the black king is not already in the corner. The theory of these rare endings was worked out by A. Troitsky, the pioneer of study composing, and is too difficult for beginners. Here we shall look at just one example so as to appreciate how the mate is accomplished once the weaker side's king is in the corner.

9

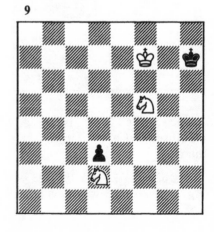

1 ♘e4 d2

1 ... ♔h8 2 ♘f6 d2 comes to the same thing.

2 ♘f6+ ♔h8 3 ♘e7 d1=♛

The irony of fate! Black has succeeded in getting a queen but is mated:

4 ♘g6 mate

2 Various Pieces in Combat

Queen versus Rook

A queen usually wins against a rook. The winning plan consists in bringing the queen and king up close to the opponent's king and rook and forcing them to separate. Then, either the rook falls to checks by the queen; or the king, deprived of the support of the rook, is mated.

Positions in which one side finds having to move a disadvantage are called, in the terminology of chess theory, *zugzwang* positions (from the German *zug* – move; *zwingen* – to compel).

The winning plan, therefore, consists in creating a zugzwang position, in which the weaker side will be compelled to move his rook away from his king – which will lead to defeat. We shall see later that obtaining a zugzwang position is an important strategic motif in many endings.

Here is a typical position.

Black is in zugzwang: he must move his rook away from his king, since against 1 ... ♔a6 the reply 2 ♕c8 is decisive, while if

10   After A.Philidor, 1777   B

1 ... ♖b8 then 2 ♕a5 mate.

On 1 ... ♖b4 both 2 ♕e7+ and 2 ♕a5+ win the rook at once, whilst if 1 ... ♖b2 or 1 ... ♖g7 then 2 ♕d4+. Therefore, the only moves worth considering are 1 ... ♖b3, 1 ... ♖f7, 1 ... ♖b1 and 1 ... ♖h7. However, in each case the white queen finally wins the rook after a series of checks.

1 ... ♖b3 is followed by 2 ♕d4+ ♔b8 3 ♕f4+ ♔a7 4 ♕a4+ and 1 ... ♖f7 by 2 ♕d4+ ♔b8 3 ♕b2+ ♔a8 4 ♕a2+.

If 1 ... ♖b1 then 2 ♕d4+ ♔b8 3 ♕h8+ ♔a7 4 ♕h7+ wins: lastly, if

16

1 ... ♖h7, then 2 ♕d4+ ♔b8 3 ♕e5+ ♔a7 4 ♕a1+ and 5 ♕b1+.

It is remarkable how, in spite of its apparent freedom, the rook always falls to the blows of the all-embracing queen.

If it is White's move, he ought not to close in on his opponent any further. Thus, 1 ♕c8 is answered by 1 ... ♖b6+, and White is obliged to retreat his king to c5, since 2 ♔c7? leads to stalemate and a draw after 2 ... ♖c6+!.

In order to win one should transfer the move to Black. This can be done in three moves:

1 ♕d4+ ♔a8 2 ♕h8+ ♔a7 3 ♕d8

Black is in zugzwang, and the rest is clear.

Analysis of the following position will acquaint one with the method of closing in on the king.

11   **W**

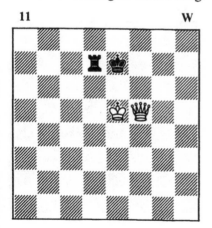

1 ♕f6+ ♔e8 2 ♕h8+

2 ♔e6 would be a mistake, for it would be followed by 2 ... ♖d6+! with an immediate draw. White must not forget about Black's stalemate possibilities.

2 ... ♔f7 3 ♕c8 ♔e7

Moving the rook away loses at once. If 3 ... ♖d3 then 4 ♕c4+ is decisive; if 3 ... ♖d2 then 4 ♕b7+ ♔e8 5 ♕b5+ ♔f7 6 ♕c4+ ♔e8 7 ♔e6 wins; and if 3 ... ♖d1, then 4 ♕c4+ ♔e7 5 ♕b4+ ♔d8 6 ♔e6. Observe how the queen carries out two tasks at the same time: it restricts the opponent's king and does not give his rook the chance to check the king from behind.

Finally, if Black plays 3 ... ♖e7+, there follows 4 ♔f5 ♔g7 (or 4 ... ♖e8 5 ♕c4+ ♔e7 6 ♕c7+ and 7 ♔f6) 5 ♕d8 ♖f7+ 6 ♔g5 ♔h7 7 ♕d4 ♖g7+ 8 ♔f6 ♔g8 9 ♕d8+ ♔h7 10 ♕e8 and we have before us Position No. 10, except that it is on the right-hand side of the board. We shall now continue our examination of the situation after the 3rd move.

4 ♕g8 ♖c7

Retreating the rook along the file loses even more quickly. On 4 ... ♖d3 and 4 ... ♖d2 the replies 5 ♕h7+ and 5 ♕g5+ are respectively decisive; while after 4 ... ♖d1 5 ♕g5+ ♔f8 (obviously, this is the only move which does not lead to

the immediate loss of the rook) 6
♕f4+ ♔e7 7 ♕h4+ ♔f8 8 ♔e6!
Black either gets mated or loses
his rook.

**5 ♕g7+ ♔d8 6 ♕f8+ ♔d7 7
♔d5! ♖b7**

Black is forced to withdraw the
rook along the rank. It is again
lost after 7 ... ♖c3 8 ♕g7+ or 7 ...
♖c2 8 ♕f5+; while if 7 ... ♖c1,
then 8 ♕f5+ ♔e8 9 ♕h5+ ♔d7 10
♕g4+ ♔e8 11 ♔d6! wins.

**8 ♕f7+ ♔c8 9 ♕e8+ ♔c7 10
♔c5 ♖a7**

The reader will no longer have
any difficulty in finding the correct
replies for White if the rook
retreats instead along the file.

**11 ♕e7+ ♔b8 12 ♕d8+ ♔b7 13
♔b5 ♖a8 14 ♕d7+ ♔b8 15 ♔b6**

Black has no satisfactory defence
against the threat of mate.

It is only in the most exceptional
circumstances that the game can
be saved with a rook against a
queen. Here is a case.

In this position Black is able to
exploit the unfortunate placing of
the white pieces and give perpetual
check.

1 ... ♖g7+ 2 ♔f5

Or 2 ♔f6 ♖g6+!.

**2 ... ♖f7+ 3 ♔g6 ♖g7+ 4 ♔h6
♖h7+!**

This is the point: if the rook is
captured, it is stalemate.

Queen versus Minor Piece

A queen wins very easily against
a minor piece.

If the opponent has a bishop,
the queen and king normally
progress via squares inaccessible
to the bishop.

12   D.Ponziani, 1782   **B**

13

1 ♕b5 ♔d6 2 ♔d4 ♗e6 3 ♕b6+
♔e7 4 ♔e5 ♗f7 5 ♕d6+ ♔e8 6
♔f6 and 7 ♕e7 mate

Driving the king back is almost
as simple a matter as in the ending
with a queen against the lone
king.

A knight defends the king
better than a bishop. However, it
too is powerless to combat such a
mighty piece as a queen.

14

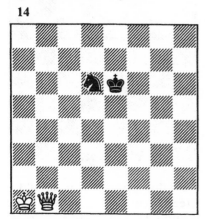

1 ♔b2 ♔d5 2 ♔c3 ♘e4+ 3 ♔d3
♘c5+ 4 ♔e3 ♘e6

Black strives to remain in the
centre as long as possible.

5 ♕f5+ ♔d6 6 ♔e4 ♘c5+ 7
♔d4 ♘e6+ 8 ♔c4 ♘c7 9 ♕c5+
♔d7 10 ♕b6 ♘e6 11 ♔d5 ♘c7+
12 ♔e5 ♘e8 13 ♕e6+ ♔d8 14 ♕f7
♘c7 15 ♔d6 ♘b5+ 16 ♔c5

Black can postpone the inevitable mate only by sacrificing his
knight.

Rook versus Knight

There is no forced win with a
rook against a knight, but the
defence requires a certain degree
of accuracy. Let us examine the
following example.

15

After White's 1 ♔f6 the only
reply for Black is 1 ... ♘h7+ as 1
... ♔h8 loses to 2 ♖e8 ♔g8 3 ♖d8.
Play continues:

2 ♔g6 ♘f8+ 3 ♔h6 ♔h8 4 ♖f7
♔g8!

4 ... ♘e6 loses at once because
of 5 ♖f6.

5 ♖g7+ ♔h8 6 ♖g1

One gets the impression that
White has achieved a great deal,
yet even so Black possesses the
resources to save the game.

6 ... ♘d7!

This is again the only reply. 6 ...

♘h7 leads to defeat after 7 ♔g6 ♔g8 (or 7 ... ♘f8+ 8 ♔f7 ♘h7 9 ♖g8 mate) 8 ♖g2 ♘f8+ 9 ♔f6+ followed by 10 ♔f7; so does 6 ... ♘e6 after 7 ♔g6 ♘f8+ 8 ♔f7.

But now 7 **♔g6** achieves nothing, as it is answered by 7 ... **♔g8! 8 ♖g2 ♔f8**. Black is also safe after 8 ♖d1 ♘f8+.

Thus, in the ending with a rook against a knight it is not dangerous for the king to be confined to the edge of the board. However, there are positions where the bad placing of the knight and king leads to a loss.

The following position was known as far back as the ninth century.

16

After 1 **♖d7 ♔b8 2 ♔b6 ♔a8 3 ♖h7 ♘d8 4 ♖h8** Black is mated next move.

This example shows that, as a rule, a knight is poorly placed when in the corner.

Another possibility of playing for a win in this ending occurs when the king and knight are separated: one can play either to win the knight or mate the king, deprived as it is of the knight's support.

17

In this position the knight is already cut off from the king. White's task, therefore, consists in preventing his opponent's force from being reunited and in trapping the knight. White, represented here by Wilhelm Steinitz, one of the strongest players of the nineteenth century, accomplished this plan in the following way:

1 ♖e4 ♘d1

If 1 ... ♘g2, then 2 ♔f6, 3 ♔g5 and 4 ♖e2, when the knight is netted; while if 1 ... ♘c2, there follows 2 ♔d5 ♘a3 3 ♔c5 ♘b1 4

♔b4 ♘d2 5 ♖f4+ ♔e7 6 ♔c3 ♘b1+ 7 ♔b2 ♘d2 8 ♔c2.

2 ♖f4+ ♔g7 3 ♖f3

The knight has been driven back and cut off from the king conclusively. Now one can proceed to catch it.

3 ... ♔g6

Alternatively, 3 ... ♘b2 4 ♔d5 ♔g6 5 ♔d4 ♔g5 6 ♖f1! ♔g4 7 ♖b1 ♘a4 8 ♖b4.

4 ♔e5 ♔g5 5 ♔d4 ♔g4 6 ♖f1 ♘b2 7 ♖b1 ♘a4 8 ♖b4

And the knight is caught.

Rook versus Bishop

The ending with a rook against a bishop usually ends in a draw. Here too, as in the case of rook versus knight, one need have no fear of being driven to the edge of the board, since even then the game can be saved with correct defence.

One thing it is important to remember: when retreating, the weaker side's king must strive to reach a corner square that is inaccessible to the bishop.

Here is an important critical position.

Black's king is in a safe corner. The reader will be able to satisfy himself that all further attempts

18   B.Horwitz and I.Kling

to restrict the black pieces lead only to stalemate.

Now let us take an example of unsuccessful defence with a bishop against a rook.

19   **B**

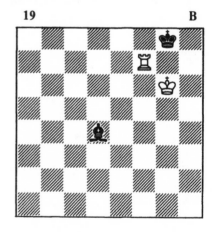

The black king is badly placed, being in a 'dangerous' corner, and so White is able to win.

1 ... ♗g1

The bishop must hide, for there was a threat of 1 ♖d7 ♗b6 2 ♖b7 ♗c5 3 ♖b8+ ♗f8 4 ♖a8 and mate next move.

2 ♖f1 ♗h2 3 ♖h1 ♗g3 4 ♖g1 ♗h2 5 ♖g2!

Despite Black's desperate defence, White has succeeded in driving the bishop out of its refuge. The rest is simple; for example

5 ... ♗e5 6 ♖e2 ♗d6 7 ♖e8+

with mate in two moves.

It may also be possible to win with a rook against a bishop when the opponent's men are separated.

In this position, representing

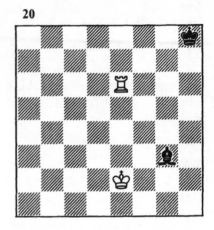

20

the conclusion of a study, White wins by **1 ♔f3**. In spite of its apparent freedom, the bishop has no good squares to which to retreat.

3 Various Pieces in Combat with a Pawn

Queen versus Pawn

A queen usually wins easily against a pawn, but there are a few exceptions. Clearly, a pawn can only compete with a queen when it is on the point of being promoted, is supported by the king, and, furthermore, the opponent's king is some distance away from it.

Let us examine, for example, the following position.

21

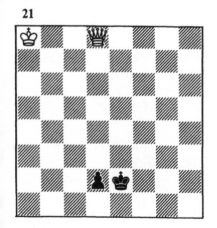

The queen alone cannot deal

with the pawn; so the result will depend on whether the white king can come to its help. Here this is possible. By means of repeated checks White compels his opponent's king to occupy the square in front of the pawn; then he brings up his own king stage by stage. The winning process is not complicated.

1 ♕e7+ ♔f2 2 ♕d6 ♔e2 3 ♕e5+ ♔f2 4 ♕d4+ ♔e2 5 ♕e4+ ♔f2 6 ♕d3

This manoeuvre could have been shortened slightly: 1 ♕e8+ ♔f2 2 ♕a4! ♔e2 3 ♕e4+ ♔f2 4 ♕d3 etc.

6 ... ♔e1 7 ♕e3+ ♔d1 8 ♔b7

As the black king has occupied the square in front of the pawn, White can now approach with his.

8 ... ♔c2 9 ♕e2 ♔c1 10 ♕c4+ ♔b2 11 ♕d3! ♔c1 12 ♕c3+ ♔d1 13 ♔c6 ♔e2 14 ♕c2 ♔e1 15 ♕e4+ ♔f2 16 ♕d3 ♔e1 17 ♕e3+ ♔d1 18 ♔d5 ♔c2 19 ♕e2 ♔c1 20 ♕c4+

23

♔b2 21 ♕d3 ♚c1 22 ♕c3+ ♚d1 23 ♔e4 ♚e2 24 ♕e3+ ♚d1 25 ♚d3

And White wins first the pawn and then the game.

As we shall see below, this method of winning is only valid with a centre pawn or a knight's pawn. The reader should also note that White began with a check on the e-file. Had the white king been on e7, e6, or e5, it would have prevented the queen from effecting its "stepped" approach and the ending would be drawn.

Victory is normally attainable in these positions if it is possible to start with a check or a pin.

In the next example the winning method employed in Position No. 21 does not work.

22

After 1 ♕d7+ ♚c1 2 ♚b7 ♚b1 3 ♕b5+ ♚a2 4 ♕c4+ ♚b2 5 ♕b4+

♚a1 6 ♕c3+ ♚b1 7 ♕b3+ Black continues with 7 ... ♚a1!.

What is White to do now? Since capturing the pawn results in stalemate, he cannot gain time to bring up his king. White would win if his king was somewhere in the vicinity of the pawn – say, on a5.

23

Then after 1 ♕d7+ ♚c1 2 ♚b4 ♚b2 3 ♕d4+ ♚b1 the reply 4 ♚b3! is possible, and although Black has time to queen his pawn (4 ... c1=♕) he gets mated by 5 ♕d3+ ♚a1 6 ♕a6+ ♚b1 7 ♕a2 mate.

Let us now examine a position with a rook's pawn.

The queen can proceed with its stepped approach:

1 ♕b7+ ♚c2 2 ♕a6 ♚b2 3 ♕b5+ ♚c2 4 ♕a4+ ♚b2 5 ♕b4+

24

♚c2 6 ♕a3 ♚b1 7 ♕b3+ ♚a1

White has forced the black king to occupy the square in front of the pawn, but it has little meaning – the king is stalemated and White cannot approach with his. As in Position No. 23, White can win if his king is somewhere in the vicinity of the pawn.

25

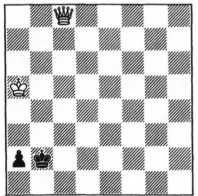

1 ♕b8+ ♚c2 2 ♕e5! ♚b1 3 ♕e1+ ♚b2 4 ♕d2+ ♚b1 5 ♚b4! a1=♕ 6 ♚b3 ♕c3+

With mate threatened, Black tries his last chance: **7 ♕xc3** stalemates him.

7 ♚xc3 and wins

If the pawn is two moves short of the queening square, there is generally no difficulty in winning by the method just examined, for the threat of stalemate is absent.

Only a few drawn positions, where the king and queen are unable to co-ordinate their actions, are known to theory.

26   *Chess World*, 1865

After **1 ♕h1+ ♚b2** White cannot prevent the pawn reaching the seventh rank because his king is badly placed. In occupying a square on the a1-h8 diagonal it interferes with the queen's manoeuvres. If the king were on f7,

White would continue with 2 ♕h8! and win easily. For example, 2 ... ♔c2 (or 2 ... ♔b3 3 ♔e6! c2 4 ♕a1!) 3 ♔e6 ♔d2 4 ♕h2+ ♔d1 5 ♕g1+ ♔d2 6 ♕d4+ ♔c2 7 ♔d5 ♔b3 8 ♔e4 c2 9 ♕a1.

Rook versus Pawn

A rook usually wins against a pawn, but the game may end in a draw if the stronger side's king is unable to support the rook in its struggle with the pawn. In very exceptional cases, where the king and rook are manifestly badly placed, the "insignificant" pawn, being on the verge of promotion, can prove more dangerous than the rook.

If the stronger side's king stands in the pawn's path or has time to approach the pawn in the course of the play, then winning is an easy matter.

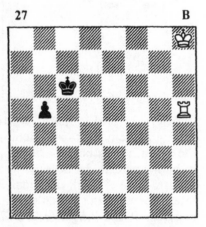

27   B

In diagram 27 Black cannot advance the pawn without the support of his king, since he would lose it. For example, 1 ... b4 2 ♔g7 b3 3 ♖h3 b2 4 ♖b3, etc.

On the other hand, if Black advances the pawn with the support of the king, then the white king has time to come to the aid of the rook:

1 ... ♔b6 2 ♔g7 ♔a5 3 ♔f6 ♔a4 4 ♔e5 b4 5 ♔d4 b3 6 ♔c3

And White wins.

It is useful to know the following rule: if the weaker side's king is behind the pawn, then to win one usually has to cut off the king with the rook on the fourth rank (reckoned from the weaker side's point of view).

28

In this position the result depends on whether the white king can occupy the d2 square as soon as the pawn reaches the second rank. If it is White's move then he is in time:

1 ♔b4 e3 2 ♔c3 e2 3 ♔d2

With Black to move, the game ends in a draw:

1 ... e3 2 ♔b4 e2 3 ♔c3 e1=♛+ etc

The next example is slightly more complicated, though the method of play is exactly the same.

29

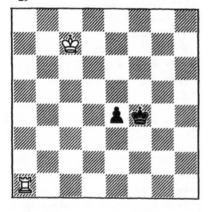

Again, everything depends on a single tempo. With the move, White is in time to stop the pawn:

1 ♔d6 e3 2 ♔d5 e2 3 ♔d4 ♔f3 4 ♔d3 ♔f2 5 ♔d2

But if Black is to move, he is saved:

1 ... e3 2 ♔d6 e2 3 ♔d5 ♔e3 4 ♔c4 ♔f2

The stronger side's king must proceed towards the pawn in such a way that the enemy king cannot interfere with it.

30

Here White has to hurry to stop the pawn.

1 ♔d6 g4

The black king is not able to hinder the progress of the opponent's king. For instance, 1 ... ♔e4 is followed by 2 ♖g7 ♔f4 3 ♔d5 g4 4 ♔d4 ♔f3 5 ♔d3 g3 6 ♖f7+ ♔g2 7 ♔e2, etc.

2 ♔d5 ♔f4 3 ♔d4 ♔f3 4 ♔d3 g3 5 ♖f7+ ♔g2 6 ♔e2 and wins.

In Position 31 White achieves nothing by approaching the pawn with his king immediately. After 1 ♔f7 e4 2 ♔e6 e3 3 ♔f5 e2 4 ♔f4 ♔d3 5 ♔f3 Black wins an important tempo by 5 ... ♔d2, thus exploiting the unfavourable position of the rook; the ending is then drawn.

31

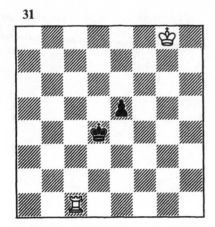

However, by playing first **1 Rd1+!** ♔c3 **2 Re1!** White can transfer his rook to a better square with gain of tempo. He then wins after **2 ... ♔d4 3 ♔f7 e4 4 ♔e6 e3 5 ♔f5 ♔d3 6 ♔f4 e2 7 ♔f3.**

One tempo decided everything! The possibility of gaining a tempo is extremely important in these endings.

32

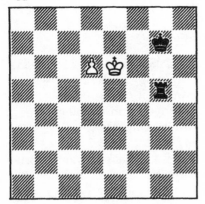

In conclusion, let us look at an example where the king and rook are badly placed.

The black king hinders the rook in its battle with the pawn, and because of this Black actually loses.

1 d7 Rg6+

As Black cannot stop the pawn, the only thing left to him is to check.

2 ♔e5!

The check with the rook was by no means as innocent as it might have seemed at first. White must play accurately. 2 ♔e7 leads to a draw because of 2 ... Rg1! 3 d8=♕ Re1+ 4 ♔d7 Rd1+; so does 2 ♔d5 Rg1 with the threat of 3 ... Rd1+.

2 ... Rg5+ 3 ♔e4 Rg4+ 4 ♔d3 Rg1 5 ♔c2

Where is the white king going? It is not hard to see that it can take cover from the checks at c7, but care is needed in crossing the d-file lest the black rook be given the tempo necessary to reach this file and save the game.

5 ... Rg2+ 6 ♔c3 Rg3+ 7 ♔c4 Rg4+ 8 ♔c5 Rg5+ 9 ♔c6 Rg6+ 10 ♔c7 and the pawn queens.

Minor Piece versus Pawn

The contest between a minor

piece and a pawn usually ends in a draw. Where the king supports the piece the result is a foregone conclusion. We shall be mainly interested in those positions in which the minor piece has to combat the pawn unaided.

We shall separately examine how a bishop and a knight cope with a pawn.

A bishop, being a long-range piece, is able to stop a pawn from a distance by attacking one of the squares in its path. Accordingly, only in exceptional cases, where not only the enemy king but also one's own interferes with it, is a bishop unable to deal with a pawn.

33

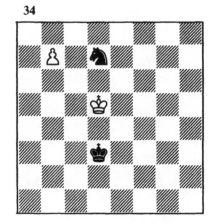

To draw the game it is enough for Black to get his bishop to one of the squares on the a7-g1 diagonal. But White plays **1 ♔e4** and answers **1 ... ♗h4** with **2 ♔f3**, after which it is clear that Black

cannot stop the pawn. If the black king had not been on f6, where it limits the bishop's manoeuvrability, but on g6, then **1 ♔e4 ♗d8 2 a6 ♗b6** would have led to a draw.

The above position is a rare exception, and in practice, as long as the pawn has not advanced too far, the bishop has time to stop it.

A knight is much worse than a bishop at dealing with a passed pawn. Nevertheless, if it is supported by the king, drawing is an elementary matter. The task is more complicated if the knight has to combat the pawn alone. Unlike a bishop, a knight cannot stop a pawn from a distance.

Provided the pawn is not a rook's pawn, the knight, without the support of the king, can stop it on the seventh rank by occupying the square in front of it.

34

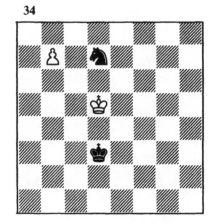

In this position play continues:

1 ♔d6 ♘b8 2 ♔c7 ♘a6+ 3 ♔b6 ♘b8

And it is clear that the enemy king is in no way able to drive the knight away from the pawn.

But in the case of the rook's pawn the knight finds itself without the necessary retreat squares; it is therefore trapped and lost.

35

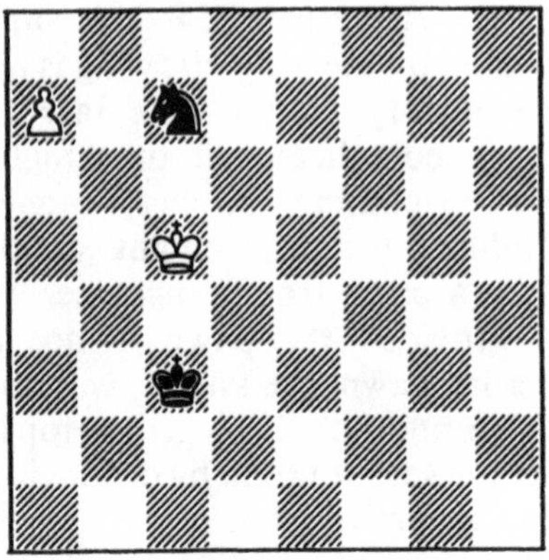

After **1 ♔c6 ♘a8 2 ♔b7** White wins the knight and with it the game. Yet, when the rook's pawn is on the sixth rank the knight copes with the situation excellently, alone or not.

No matter how White continues in Position 36, he is unable to drive the knight away from the pawn. For example:

1 ♔c5 ♘a7 2 ♔b6 ♘c8+ 3 ♔b7 ♘d6+ 4 ♔c7 ♘b5+ 5 ♔b6

Apparently, White has suc-

36

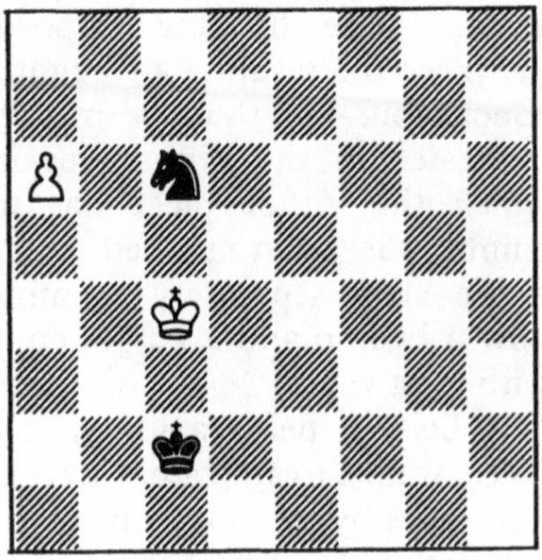

ceeded in driving off the knight, but Black replies **5 ... ♘d6!**, whereupon 6 a7 is unsufficient on account of 6 ... ♘c8+. In this threat lies the guarantee of Black's successful defence. By 'hopping around' beside the pawn, the knight prevents it from advancing. A knight's capacity for effecting "insidious" forks is an important tactical resource in these endings.

37 **B**

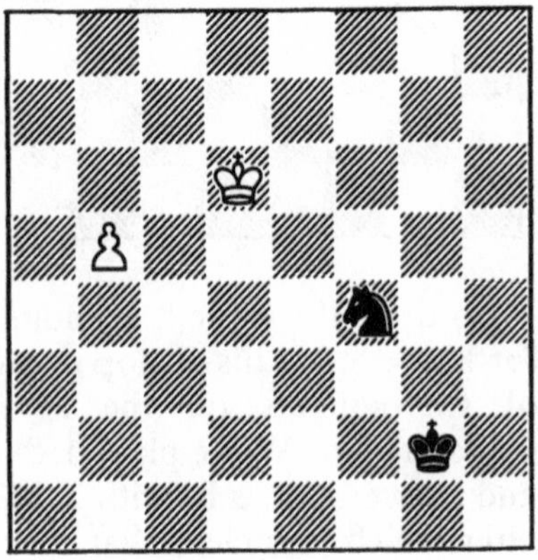

The next example shows how a knight can catch up with a pawn from afar.

In order to stop the pawn the knight must reach either b7 or b8. It cannot approach the pawn from the right, as the enemy king obstructs it. That means it must come round from the left:

1 ... ♘d3! 2 b6

If 2 ♔d5, Black can play 2 ... ♔f3 3 ♔d4 ♘f4! 4 b6 ♘e6+ and 5 ... ♘d8.

2 ... ♘b4 3 b7 ♘a6, with a draw.

Sometimes, when it would seem that the knight has no time to overhaul the pawn, the enemy king itself may help it.

38   **B**

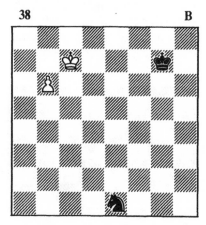

In this position Black saves himself as follows:

1 ... ♘d3 2 b7 ♘c5 3 b8=♛

♘a6+ and draws. The position of the white king came to Black's rescue. Had it stood somewhere in the background, the pawn would have queened safely.

The reader will find it useful to remember this important property of a knight – the ability to gain a necessary tempo by means of a check. The following study provides a beautiful illustration of a knight's possibilities.

39   N.Grigoriev, 1938
(Conclusion of study)

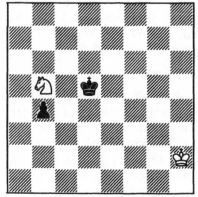

White's king is far away, so his knight must combat the opponent's forces alone. An attempt to bring up the king to its aid fails to achieve its object: after 1 ♔g2 ♔c5 followed by 2 ... b3 the knight, having been driven off, is unable to stop the pawn.

Let us try to break the position down to its essentials. White draws if his knight reaches one of the three squares a3, c3, or d2 when the pawn is on b2. But how is this to be achieved?

1 ♘c7+

First, it is necessary to improve the position of the knight and determine that of the opponent's king.

1 ... ♔c4!

This is undoubtedly the most dangerous reply for White. On 1 ... ♔d4 White could start bringing up his king by 2 ♔g2, since 2 ... b3 would be followed by 3 ♘b5+ and 4 ♘a3; while on 1 ... ♔c6 he could play 2 ♘e6 ♔b5 3 ♘d4+ ♔c4 4 ♘c6! b3 5 ♘a5+.

2 ♘e8!

A remarkable move! The knight seems to be going right away from the pawn, but in fact that is not so. The knight takes a step back only in order to come forward again afterwards. The e8 square is an important focal point. White will select the knight's route to b1 according to the position of the black king: it may be either e8-c7-b5-a3 or e8-f6-e4-d2. If now 2 ... b3, there follows 3 ♘d6+ ♔b4 (or 3 ... ♔d3 4 ♘b5 b2 5 ♘a3) 4 ♘e4 b2 5 ♘d2; for that reason the black king tries to deprive the knight of the d6 square.

2 ... ♔c5 3 ♘f6! ♔d4 4 ♘e8!

Again it goes to the focal square!

4 ... ♔e5

White is in time to stop the pawn after 4 ... b3 5 ♘d6 ♔c3 6 ♘e4+! ♔c2 7 ♘d6! b2 8 ♘c4!

5 ♘c7! ♔d6 6 ♘e8+

The one saving reply. Moving towards the pawn led to a loss: 6 ♘b5+? ♔c5 7 ♘c7 b3 8 ♘e6+ ♔c4, and the pawn queens.

6 ... ♔c5 7 ♘f6! ♔d4 8 ♘e8! b3 9 ♘d6 ♔c3 10 ♘e4+! ♔c2 11 ♘d6! b2 12 ♘c4! b1=♕ 13 ♘a3+ with a draw.

The knight demonstrates its capabilities like a virtuoso. We recommend the reader to examine this study carefully.

There is another important property of a knight with which it is worth being acquainted: this is its ability to set up a 'barrier' across the path of the enemy king.

40

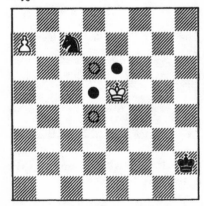

This would appear to be an elementary position in every respect. White's pawn is on the verge of promotion. The black king is a long way from the pawn and, evidently, cannot help the knight; the latter, therefore, must combat the pawn unaided. But a knight alone cannot cope with a rook's pawn on the seventh rank. White attacks the knight, drives it away from the pawn, and finally queens the pawn.

That would, indeed, be the case, were it not for one "but": namely, but for the barrier across the path of the white king that considerably lengthens the route to the pawn. In fact, if you look more deeply into the position, it becomes clear that White cannot attack the knight directly, since 1 ♔d6 is answered by 1 ... ♘b5+ and 2 ... ♘xa7. The d4, d5, d6 and e6 squares are inaccessible to the king and represent a 'barrier' across its path. Accordingly, it is forced to take a longer, roundabout route to the pawn, and in the meantime Black's king is able to come up to the aid of the knight.

Play continues thus:

1 ♔f6 ♔g3 2 ♔e7 ♔f4 3 ♔d7 ♘a8 4 ♔c8 ♔e5 5 ♔b7 ♔d6

The knight sacrifices itself and the white king is caught in the 'prison'.

6 ♔xa8 ♔c7 stalemate

Here is another important drawn position.

41

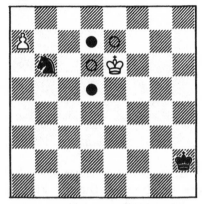

Again a barrier has been set up across the path of the white king. The d5, d6, d7 and e7 squares are inaccessible, and it must go on a circuitous route of either e5-d4-c5-c6-b7 or f7-e8-d8-c7-b7. In both cases it takes five moves to reach b7, and Black has time, by sacrificing the knight at a8, to get his king to c7 and stalemate his opponent.

Once one has become acquainted with these two positions, it is not difficult to solve the following study.

How is White to save the day? The knight cannot catch the pawn by direct means; for instance, 1 ♘g6 h3 2 ♘f4 h2 3 ♘e2+ ♔d2 4 ♘g3 ♔e1 5 ♔d6 ♔f2 and Black wins.

42   N.Grigoriev, 1932

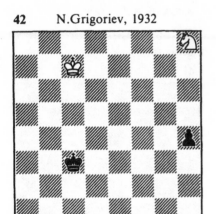

But is it not possible to exploit the position of Black's king in order to catch the pawn? Knowing this idea, one can easily find the correct knight manoeuvre.

1 ♘f7 h3 2 ♘g5 h2 3 ♘e4+

This gives White the possibility of stopping the pawn by either 4 ♘g3 or 4 ♘f2. The right choice depends on which direction the black king takes. Thus, if 3 ... ♚d3, then 4 ♘g3! is the only move; while if 3 ... ♚d4, only 4 ♘f2! is sufficient. Both set up a 'barrier' across the path of the opponent's king.

Black's best plan, therefore, is to start out on the detour immediately and play **3 ... ♚c2**. If White now replies 4 ♘f2, he loses after 4 ... ♚d2 5 ♚d6 ♚e2 6 ♘h1

♚f3 7 ♚e5 ♚g2. However, by continuing **4 ♘g3! ♚d1 5 ♚d6 ♚e1 6 ♚e5 ♚f2 7 ♚f4** White is in time to protect the knight and force a draw.

The reader will be interested to learn, I am sure, that one is not always obliged to defend with a knight against a pawn. If, in the case of a rook's pawn, the enemy king is in the corner, blocked by its own pawn, it is sometimes possible to construct a mating net around it.

Here is one of these exceptional positions.

43

This position was known as long ago as the twelfth century. White plays and mates in three moves:

1 ♘b4+ ♚a1 2 ♚c1 a2 3 ♘c2 mate

4 Queening a Pawn

In the endgame an extra "insignificant" pawn may be decisive, since, promoted to a queen, it will furnish a material superiority sufficient for mate.

Our analysis in this chapter covers the following points: how to advance and promote a pawn with various pieces present; when it is possible to queen a pawn and when not; which factors contribute to and which hinder pawn promotion.

King and Pawn versus King

The king combats a pawn best of all when it occupies one of the squares in its path or, as we usually say, when it blockades it. However, the king cannot remain on this square forever. On its turn to move it is compelled to retreat a step, leave the square free, and give way to the pawn. A pawn supported by the king will move forward, until finally it all comes down to the following critical situation, in which the defending king no longer has anywhere to retreat.

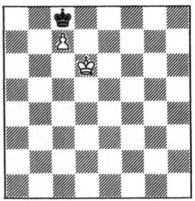

44

We have here a typical mutual zugzwang position. The right to move is unfavourable for both sides. White would have to play 1 ♔c6, conceding stalemate and a draw; whilst Black, if it were his turn, would be obliged to continue 1 ... ♔b7, against which White replies 2 ♔d7 and queens his pawn. This means that White, in advancing the pawn, must strive to get this position with Black to move; Black the same with White to move.

Let us attempt to define when this is possible. Consider a position with a white pawn on c5.

35

45

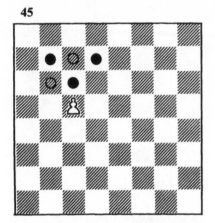

It is clear that if the white king succeeds in occupying one of the three squares, b7, c7 and d7, in front of the pawn, White will queen the pawn automatically. Now let us try to determine what the result will be with the white king on d6. If Black's king is then on c8, the turning manoeuvre **1 ♔c6 ♔d8** (or 1 ... ♔b8 2 ♔d7) **2 ♔b7** decides the game. If the black king stands on d8, then **1 c6 ♔c8 2 c7 ♔b7 3 ♔d7** is decisive.

Continuing our analysis further, we easily establish that White also wins if his king is able to occupy c6 or b6, regardless of where the black king is situated.

These six squares (b7, c7, d7, b6, c6 and d6 in the case of a pawn at c5) are called – in the theory of pawn endings – key squares, since the occupation of any one of them by the white king leads to the

attainment of White's ends (the promotion of the pawn).

Black draws the ending if he is able to prevent the white king from reaching the key squares. It is easy to see that with the white king on d5 Black must have his king on either d7 or c7 in order to draw; while if White's king is on b5, then Black's must be on either b7 or c7. Then, after **1 c6**, Black has to move his king back in such a way that 2 ♔b6 and 2 ♔d6 can be answered by 2 ... ♔b8 and 2 ... ♔d8 respectively. With his king on c7, therefore, Black has only one reply that saves the game, and that is **1 ... ♔c8**; this meets the requirements laid down, whereas 1 ... ♔d8 (or 1 ... ♔b8) leads to zugzwang and a loss for Black after 2 ♔d6 (or 2 ♔b6) 2 ... ♔c8 3 c7.

Below is another important mutual zugzwang position. Here the key squares are b4, c4, and d4.

46

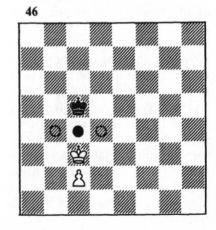

Let us verify this. Suppose that it is Black's move. He is forced to continue **1 ...** ♚b5 (or 1 ... ♚d5) whereupon White replies **2** ♔d4 (or 2 ♔b4). Now the pawn queens automatically; for example:

2 ... ♚c6 **3** ♔c4 ♚b6 **4** ♔d5 (turning) **4 ...** ♚c7 **5** ♔c5 ♚d7 **6** ♔b6

Having carried out the turning manoeuvre with his king and occupied one of the basic key squares, White can begin to advance the pawn.

It is another matter if it is White's move. Black answers **1** ♔b3 with **1 ...** ♚b5 (or if 1 ♔d3, then 1 ... ♚d5) preventing the advance of of the white king. After **2** c4+ ♚c5 **3** ♔c3 ♚c6 (both 3 ... ♚d6 and 3 ... ♚b6 are also possible) **4** ♔d4 ♚d6 **5** c5+ ♚d7 **6** ♔d5 ♚c7 **7** c6 ♚c8! **8** ♔d6 ♚d8!, as we already know, Black draws the game.

So runs the battle for key squares.

Black's success in preventing his opponent's king from reaching one of the three key squares was achieved by the only possible method – by placing his own king opposite the enemy king or, as we normally say, by taking the opposition. The opposition of the kings represents the sole means of contesting three key squares situated side by side on one line.

As we shall see again more than once, the kings' struggle for control of key squares is a *leitmotiv* of the majority of pawn endings.

47

Let us try to solve this position by proceeding from the theory of key squares. The key squares (in relation to the pawn at c3) are d5, c5 and b5. This means that with White's king on d4 Black's king must be on d6; on c6 when White's is on c4; and on b6, when it is on b4. The White king can reach each of these three squares in three moves, while the black king reaches d6 in two moves, c6 in three and b6 in four.

If the white king makes for b4 at once, the black king is not in time to occupy the square essential in the fight for the key squares, namely b6, and Black loses. Thus the solution is revealed.

1 ♔c2! ♚e7 **2** ♔b3! ♚d6 **3** ♔b4!

♔c6 4 ♔c4!

Black is in zugzwang, and White, by laying hold of one of the key squares, gains the decision.

The fight for the key squares varies in character according to the file on which the pawn stands. In the case of a knight's pawn one must be careful even after gaining control of the key squares – stalemate is possible.

48

Here the careless 1 b6+? leads to a draw after 1 ... ♔a8, for the reply 2 ♔c7 leaves Black without any moves. The correct continuation is 1 ♔c7! ♔a8 2 ♔b6 ♔b8 3 ♔a6 ♔a8 4 b6 ♔b8 5 b7, and White wins.

Where a rook's pawn is concerned, if the enemy king occupies one of the squares in its path, then, owing to the possibility of stalemate, there is no means at all of driving it away. However, key squares do exist in the case of a rook's pawn, and their occupation by the stronger side's king guarantees the pawn's promotion. Such are the squares g7 and g8 in the following position.

49

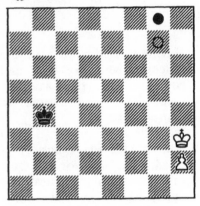

The assessment of this position depends on whose move it is. If it is White's, then he has time to get his king to g7 and win. After 1 ♔g4 ♔c5 2 ♔g5 ♔d6 3 ♔g6 ♔e7 4 ♔g7 Black cannot prevent the advance of the pawn to the queening square.

With Black to move, it is a different picture.

1 ... ♔c5 2 ♔g4 ♔d6 3 ♔f5 ♔e7 4 ♔g6 ♔f8 5 ♔h7

White is obliged to play this, as otherwise the black king gets to h8, a square from which it cannot be driven away.

5 ... ♔f7 6 h4 ♔f8 7 h5 ♔f7 8 h6

f8

Now White must choose which way he is going to draw: either he stalemates his own king or his opponent's.

Let us now consider a position where both kings are at a distance from the pawn.

50

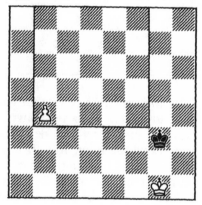

Here, too, the result depends on whose move it is. If it is White's he queens his pawn:

1 b5 **f4 2 b6** **e5 3 b7** **d6 4 b8=♛**

If it is Black's move, he has time to overtake the pawn with his king:

1 ... **f4 2 b5** **e5 3 b6** **d6 4 b7** **c7**

In order to determine quickly whether the king can overtake the pawn or not in these endings the so-called 'rule of the square' is employed. On the diagram the square of the pawn (i.e. b4-b8-f8-f4) is traced in a thick line.

The rule of the square consists in the following: if the king is in the square of the pawn or can enter it on the move, then it overtakes the pawn; if not, it cannot catch up. With a pawn in its initial position, when it has the right to advance two squares at once, the square is formed on the basis of the pawn's already being on the third rank.

King, Minor Piece and Pawn versus King

As king and minor piece cannot mate the enemy king, all one's hopes here are pinned on the pawn. It must be queened and thereby guarantee the material advantage necessary for mate. This is usually an elementary task, but there are a few exceptional positions in which, despite the overwhelming material superiority, the win proves unattainable. It is with these positions that we wish to acquaint the reader.

(see diagram 51)

The white pawn has reached the seventh and penultimate rank, but it cannot take the one remaining step: Black's king impedes it, and there is no way of driving it out of the corner. For example

51

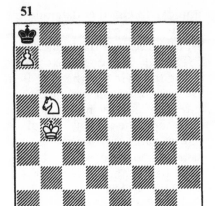

1 ♔c5 ♔b7 2 ♔d6 ♔a8 3 ♔c6 stalemate

The white knight could also be on c6 or c8.

Were the pawn on the sixth rank, White would win without any trouble.

52

1 ♔c4 ♔b6 2 ♔d5 ♔a7 3 ♔c6 ♔a8 4 ♔b6 ♔b8 5 ♘d5 ♔a8 6

♘c7+ ♔b8 7 a7+ and 8 a8=♕

53

In this position White's own king interferes with the pawn's promotion. Everything depends here on whose move it is. If it is White's, then his king is able to break out of its prison: **1 ♘d3 ♔f8 2 ♘e5 ♔e7 3 ♔g7** and White wins.

However, with Black to move, the white king is condemned to "life imprisonment" for after **1 ... ♔f8 2 ♘d3 ♔f7 3 ♘e5+ ♔f8**, the knight is forced to concede the black king the f7 square. When we acquainted ourselves with the properties of a knight, we noted that on its own it is unable to win a tempo. For victory White needs only to transfer the move to Black, but this he cannot accomplish. It is therefore a draw.

There is a rule pertaining to this type of position, and knowing it, one can quickly adjust oneself to a given situation. The weaker side draws if it is able to move the king to the first or second rank square on the bishop's file of the same colour as that on which the knight stands.

There are also drawn positions with a bishop, and one of these is shown on the following diagram.

54 Ponziani, 1782

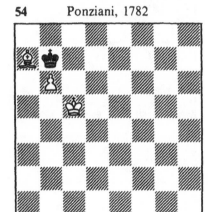

55

squared bishop, there would be no saving Black. For example, with the bishop on d3, White could continue 1 ♗e4+ ♚b8 2 a6 ♚c8 3 a7 – queening the pawn has presented no difficulties.

A knowledge of the positions examined above is essential and will enable one to avoid many mistakes.

The cause of White's failure to win is the bad position of his bishop. Because of this he cannot drive the opponent's king out of the corner.

Diagram 55 is another case where White's bishop cannot help to drive the black king out of the corner, and this task is beyond the powers of the white king alone.

The reader would do well to note that the white bishop is unable to attack the pawn's queening square. Were it a white-

56

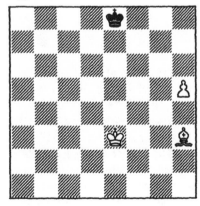

In this position it is enough for the black king to reach the h8 corner to draw, but White cuts it off by a series of precise moves and gains the decision. This happens as follows: **1 ♗e6!** (1 h6 ♔f7 leads to a draw) **1 ... ♔e7 2 h6! ♔f6 3 ♗f5! ♔f7 4 ♗h7! ♔f6 5 ♔f4 ♔f7 6 ♔g5 ♔f8 7 ♔f6 ♔e8 8 ♔g7** and White queens the pawn.

Sometimes it is necessary to sacrifice the piece in order to preserve the pawn. Let us consider two examples (see diagrams 57 and 58):

57

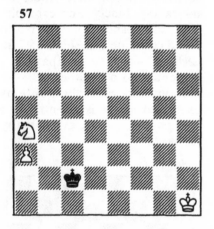

Black threatens to attack the pawn and win it. How is White to continue? The natural moves 1 ♘b6 and 1 ♘c5 lead to a draw only. For instance, 1 ♘b6 ♔b3 2 a4 ♔b4 3 ♔g2 ♔a5 or 1 ♘c5 ♔c3 2 ♔g2 ♔c4 and, after the knight moves away, 3 ... ♔b3. Sacrificing the knight is the sole way of

winning:

1 ♘b2! ♔b3 2 a4

This device (the defence of a pawn by a knight from behind) has immense significance when the king is far off and cannot support the pawn.

58

Here, too, there is but one way to win: **1 ♗d5**, and if **1 ... ♔xd5**, then **2 ♔b5**.

Knight and Pawn versus Knight

The defending king can best contend with the pawn if it is in its path, but even then it must receive active support from the knight.

In diagram 59 the black king is compelled to do battle with the white forces on its own.

59

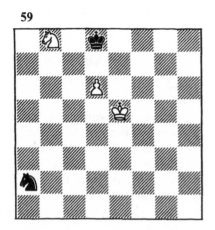

60 **B**

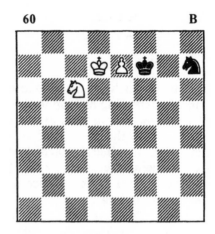

1 ♔e6 ♘b4

2 ♘c6+ was threatened, so the knight hastens to lend help. But it is already too late.

2 d7 ♔c7 3 ♘a6+!

The decisive blow! White could not play at once 3 ♔e7 on account of the reply 3 ... ♘d5+, which draws. Therefore, he first deflects the enemy knight.

3 ... ♘xa6 4 ♔e7 and the pawn cannot be stopped.

If the pawn is but a single step from promotion, the only way to save the game, as a rule, is by perpetual check.

In Position 60 Black draws by **1 ... ♘f8+ 2 ♔d8** (if 2 ♔d6 then 2 ... ♘g6) **2 ... ♘e6+.** But if the white knight could have helped to defend the king against the perpetual check, White would have won.

Let us examine a position where White's knight controls the e6 square.

61 **B**

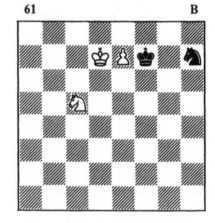

1 ... ♘f6+

Black is forced to defend passively.

2 ♔d8 ♘e8 3 ♘e6! ♘d6

Or 3 ... ♘f6 4 ♘g5+ and 5 ♘e4,

deflecting the enemy knight.

4 ♔d7 ♘e8 5 ♘g5+

And White wins.

Thus, in such positions White wins by deflecting his opponent's pieces away from the area of conflict with the pawn, and this deflection is generally achieved by sacrificing the knight. Knight sacrifices are a typical device in analogous endings.

If the pawn is not threatening to promote at once, the weaker side's chances of saving the game are noticeably improved.

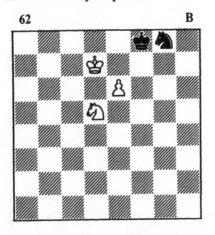

62   B

We have here a typical drawn position. The main role in the struggle against the pawn is entrusted to the knight. The king manoeuvres around the knight and only enters the fray when it is necessary. For example:

1 ... ♔g7 2 ♔e8 ♘h6! 3 ♘e7

Or 3 e7 ♘f5.

3 ... ♔f6 4 ♔d7 ♔g7 5 ♘d5 ♘g8

And White has achieved nothing.

However, if you consider a position similar to the previous one but with all the pieces moved a file to the right, then Black is no longer able to save the game, since on the edge of the board his men lack the space in which to manoeuvre.

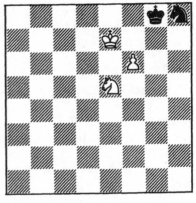

63   After A.Chéron, 1952

In this case White is able to drive the black king away. For example:

1 ... ♔h7 2 ♔f8 ♔h6 3 ♔g8 ♔g5 4 ♔g7 ♔f5 5 ♘d7 ♘g6

Black is forced to allow the pawn to advance. The rest we already know.

6 f7 ♔g5 7 ♘e5! ♘f4! 8 ♔g8 ♘e6 9 ♘f3+ and 10 ♘d4

White deflects the enemy knight by the now familiar device.

The nearer a pawn is to one of the rook's files the more dangerous it becomes for the knight, as proximity to the edge of the board considerably lessens a knight's fighting capacity. To satisfy ourselves of this, let us examine some positions which feature a rook's pawn.

64

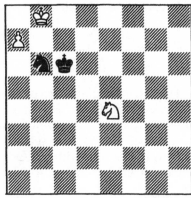

Black threatens to force a draw by perpetual check by 1 ... ♘d7+. But with the move, White wards off this threat and wins easily.

1 ♘f6 ♘a8!

This is the only possibility of putting up a resistance. After 1 ... ♔c5 2 ♔b7 ♔b5 3 ♘d5! White drives the knight away.

2 ♘d5!

Of course, not 2 ♔xa8 ♔c7, when Black draws.

2 ... ♔d7 3 ♔b7 ♔d8 4 ♘b6 ♘c7 5 ♔c6 and wins.

In the next position the winning line is considerably more complicated.

65   R.Réti, 1929

If it is Black's move, his knight gets driven off by White in the following way: 1 ... ♔b4 2 ♔b6 ♔c4 3 ♘c3! ♘d6 4 ♔c7 ♔c5 5 a7, and wins. Playing first, therefore, White needs to transfer the move to his opponent in order to win. This he succeeds in doing by means of an ingenious manoeuvre.

1 ♘c5!

Against other knight moves Black continues 1 ... ♘d6+ 2 ♔a7 ♘c8+, securing the draw.

1 ... ♔b4

White's task is simplified by the continuation 1 ... ♘d6+ 2 ♔c7 ♘b5+ 3 ♔c6! ♘a7+ 4 ♔b7 ♘b5 5 ♘e4, when his object is achieved.

2 ♔b6 ♘d6 3 ♘e4! ♘c8+ 4 ♔c7!

Necessary precision! White avoids the concealed hazard 4 ♔b7 ♔b5 after which Black saves the game, e.g. 5 ♘c3+ ♔a5 6 ♘e4 ♔b5 7 ♘f6 ♘d6+ 8 ♔a7 ♘c8+, etc.

4 ... ♔b5 5 ♔b7 ♔a5 6 ♘c5 ♘d6+ 7 ♔c7 ♘b5+ 8 ♔c6 ♘a7+ 9 ♔b7 ♘b5 10 ♘e4

White has carried out his plan. Normally, it is always possible to drive the weaker side's pieces away and promote the pawn in positions of this type, though the technical difficulties may be greater in some than others. A drawn result is feasible only in the most exceptional cases, and one of these we give below (see diagram 66).

If the white knight were on c5, then 1 ♔b8 ♘b5 2 ♔b7 would lead to the previous position after the move 1 ♘c5, where White wins. But here the knight stands on c7, interfering with White's king manoeuvre. This is the decisive factor: White cannot win.

Let us verify this:

66   R.Réti, 1929

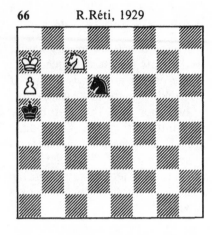

1 ♔b8 ♘b5! 2 ♔b7 ♘d6+ 3 ♔a7

Or 3 ♔c6 ♘b5!.

3 ... ♘f7!

The defence requires exceptional accuracy from Black. His knight now occupies an important focal position: if 4 ♔b8 or 4 ♔a8, he intends to continue with 4 ... ♘d8, while if 4 ♔b7 then 4 ... ♘d6+.

4 ♘e6

White attempts to regroup, but Black is able to prevent this.

4 ... ♔b5!

After 4 ... ♘d6? 5 ♘c5 ♘b5+ 6 ♔b7 White would win.

5 ♘d4+ ♔a5 6 ♘c6+ ♔b5 7 ♘b4! ♘d8!

Again Black produces the most precise move. 7 ... ♔xb4 8 ♔b8!

♘e5 9 ♔c7 leads to his defeat, as White queens the pawn.

8 ♔b8 ♘c6+ 9 ♔b7 ♘a5+ 10 ♔c7 ♘c6! and draws.

To conclude, here is another position which ranks as an exception.

67   A.Chéron, 1952

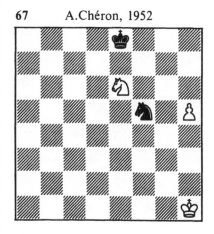

The pawn proceeds to queen by itself in spite of the fact that the opponent's pieces are stationed close by.

1 ♘g7+!

This unexpected stroke decides the game, as after **1 ... ♘xg7 2 h6 ♔f8 3 h7** Black's knight merely prevents his king from getting at the pawn.

Bishop and Pawn versus Bishop

If the bishops are of opposite colours, the defence is not at all difficult for the weaker side. Either the king must occupy a square in front of the pawn that is inaccessible to the enemy bishop or the bishop must gain control of one of the squares in the pawn's path. Only sometimes, when one's pieces are unfavourably placed, may certain difficulties arise.

68   J.Berger, 1922   **B**

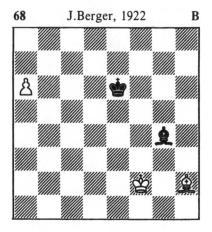

Black's position seems critical. How is he to stop the pawn? After 1 ... ♗f5 2 ♔f3 ♔d5 3 a7 ♗e4+ 4 ♔e3 it cannot be halted.

However, that does not represent Black's best defence. By continuing **1 ... ♗f5 2 ♔f3 ♗d3! 3 a7 ♗c4!**, he allows **4 a8=♕** but then wins the new-born queen by **4 ... ♗d5+**. White could also play differently, e.g. **2 ♔e3 ♗h3 3 ♔f3**, but that too leads to a draw after **3 ... ♗f1! 4 a7 ♗c4!** and **5 ... ♗d5+**.

Where bishops of the same

colour are concerned, it is a quite obvious draw if the weaker side's king succeeds in occupying a square in front of the pawn that is inaccessible to the bishop.

If the weaker side's king is unable to occupy a square in front of the pawn, the task of defence is much more complicated.

69

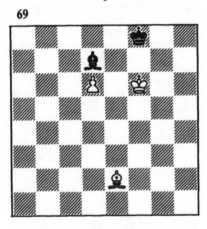

With the move, Black draws by playing 1 ... ♔e8 and getting his king to d8. So naturally, if it is White's move, he continues 1 ♗h5, preventing the passage of the king. Let us look at some possible variations arising after Black's reply 1 ... ♗h3.

2 ♗g6 ♗d7!

2 ... ♗g4 loses in view of 3 ♗f5 ♗xf5 4 ♔xf5 ♔f7 5 ♔e5 ♔f8 6 ♔f6! ♔e8 7 ♔e6 ♔d8 8 d7.

3 ♗f5 ♔e8

And Black draws.

Can White drive off the enemy bishop? To do so it is necessary for him to get his king to c7. First suppose that Black keeps to passive tactics.

2 ♔e5 ♗d7 3 ♔d5 ♗a4 4 ♔c5 ♗d7 5 ♔b6 ♗a4 6 ♔c7 ♗b5

70

We have reached a position where White is able to drive the bishop off and queen his pawn.

7 ♗f3 ♗a4

Or 7 ... ♔e8 8 ♗c6+ ♗xc6 9 ♔xc6 ♔d8 10 d7.

8 ♗c6 ♗xc6 9 ♔xc6 ♔e8 10 ♔c7 and wins.

Had Black played 5 ... ♗f5 (or another square on that diagonal) White would have won by transferring his bishop to c8 and forcing Black to let the pawn through just the same.

Thus, passive defence lost for

Black. His bishop was outnumbered and could not contend with the enemy forces alone. White carried out a typical manoeuvre, intercepting or driving off the opponent's bishop.

Is Black in a position to obstruct the manoeuvre driving off the bishop? White effected the interception by the move ♗c6, and Black could have prevented this only if his king had been on c5. It is not hard to establish that queening the pawn would be beyond White's powers in that case.

71

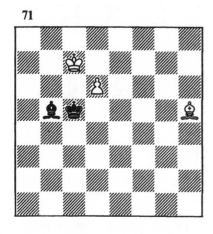

For example, 1 ♗g4 ♗a4 2 ♗d7 ♗d1 3 ♗c6 ♗g4 and White has not improved his position.

Let us now return to diagram 69. The black king has no need to look on passively at the turn of events when its opposite number makes for c7; it must itself hasten towards the square c5. After 2 ♔e5, therefore, it is imperative to continue 2 ... ♔g7 3 ♔d5 ♔f6 4 ♔c6 ♔e5 5 ♔c7 ♔d4 6 ♗e8 ♔c5, and Black has achieved his object.

However, control over the square of interception does not always save the weaker side. It is important that the bishop should also have room to work in. If the mobility of the bishop is limited, a zugzwang position may arise.

72

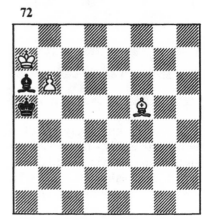

In this position the black bishop is very limited in its actions. By a simple waiting move with his bishop on the h3-c8 diagonal White puts Black in zugzwang and wins the game.

There is an important rule for positions of this type. The weaker side draws only if there are not less than three free squares on the diagonal from which its bishop controls the advance of the pawn.

In the example given there were two in all, and so White was able to win.

Here is another position confirming this rule.

73   L.Centurini, 1847

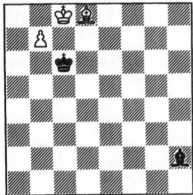

If White's king were on a8, he would win easily – by transferring his bishop to b8 via a7 and driving off Black's bishop. But the white king is less favourably placed, and Black can try to prevent the enemy bishop from getting to a7. On 1 ♗h4 he continues 1 ... ♔b5! 2 ♗f2 ♔a6!

How is White to proceed now? If he plays the waiting move 3 ♗e3, Black replies 3 ... ♗d6! 4 ♗g5 ♔b5 5 ♗d8 ♔c6 and his king has reached c6 in time. Nevertheless, White has a way of winning. It starts with 3 ♗c5!, depriving Black of his important square.

Now after 3 ... ♗f4 there follows 4 ♗e7 ♔b5 5 ♗d8 ♔c6

6 ♗g5!

Winning a tempo like this is the whole point.

6 ... ♗h2 7 ♗e3

And the bishop reaches a7.

A knowledge of the critical positions just examined is very important, and without it one will not find the correct way to draw or win in more complex positions.

Here is a typical example from grandmaster practice.

Capablanca-Janowski
74   New York 1916   B

In this position Black decided that resistance was hopeless and resigned. Yet, given correct defence, there is no way of winning here, though great resourcefulness and accuracy is demanded of the weaker side. The black king must go round behind the pawn and so prevent the bishop's diagonal from being cut.

Thus,

1 ... ♔f4!! 2 ♗d4

If 2 ♗e5+, Black plays 2 ... ♔e3 3 b5 ♔d3 4 ♔c6 ♔c4 with a clear draw.

2 ... ♔f3!! 3 b5

Or 3 ♗c5 ♔e2!! 4 ♔c6 ♔d3 5 ♔d7 ♗g5 6 b5 ♔c4.

3 ... ♔e2!!

The black king is relentless.

4 ♔c6 ♔d3 5 ♗b6 ♗g5 6 ♔b7!

The most dangerous continuation.

6 ... ♔c4 7 ♔a6 ♔b3!! 8 ♗f2 ♗d8 9 ♗e1 ♔a4!!

And the king arrives in time.

And finally, let us consider the following position, which is an exception to the rule.

75 L.Centurini, 1856

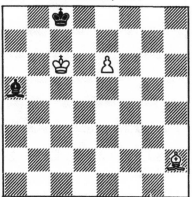

Apparently, White can queen his pawn by playing **1 e7**. But this is answered by **1 ... ♗d8!**, and if White promotes to a queen or a rook, Black is stalemated.

A draw also results both from 2 e8=♗ ♗a5! 3 ♗g3 ♔d8 followed by 4 ... ♔e7 and from 2 e8=♘ ♗h4! 3 ♗c7 ♗e7 4 ♘g7 ♗d8 5 ♗f4 ♗c7.

Bishop and Pawn versus Knight

In order to obtain a draw in the ending of bishop and pawn versus bishop it was enough for the weaker side's king to occupy one of the squares in front of the pawn that was inaccessible to the bishop. In this ending this proviso is not sufficient. It is important that the knight should not be deprived of mobility, as that may lead to zugzwang.

76

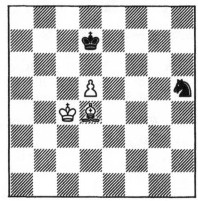

Thus in this position, after 1 ♗e5! the black knight finds itself 'fettered'; Black is in zugzwang and must allow the pawn to advance, for example:

1 ... ♔e7 2 ♔c5 ♔d7 3 d6

A small finesse. 3 ♔b6 leads to a draw after 3 ... ♘f6! 4 ♗xf6 ♔d6.

3 ... ♔e6 4 ♔c6 ♔xe5 5 d7, and White wins.

Now let us examine some positions where the weaker side's king is unable to block the pawn.

77

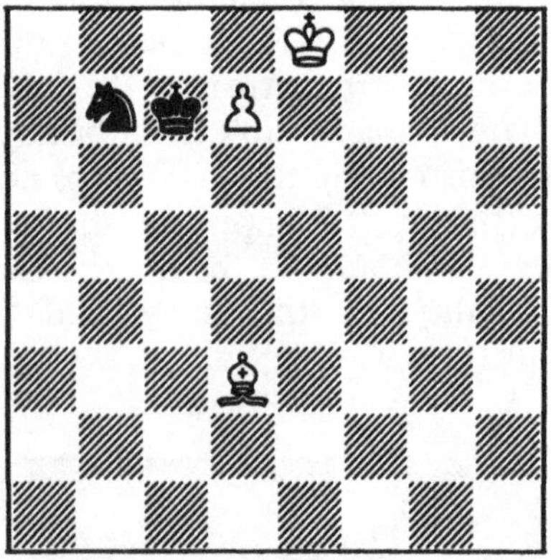

The result here depends on whose move it is. If it is Black's, then he gives perpetual check:

1 ... ♘d6+ 2 ♔e7 ♘c8+! 3 ♔e8

Or 3 ♔e6 ♘b6.

3 ... ♘d6+

That it should be drawn is to a large extent accidental, being caused by the unfavourable position of the white king.

If it is White's move, he has time to improve the position of his king and so achieve victory.

1 ♔e7! ♘d8 2 ♗e4! ♘f7 3 ♗f3 ♘d8 4 ♗d5!

By a simple bishop manoeuvre White has deprived the knight of mobility and placed his opponent in zugzwang. The winning method is typical for these positions.

It is useful to note that with a bishop's pawn the limiting of the knight's mobility leads only to stalemate. The position with a bishop's pawn is therefore an exception in which the stronger side cannot win.

78

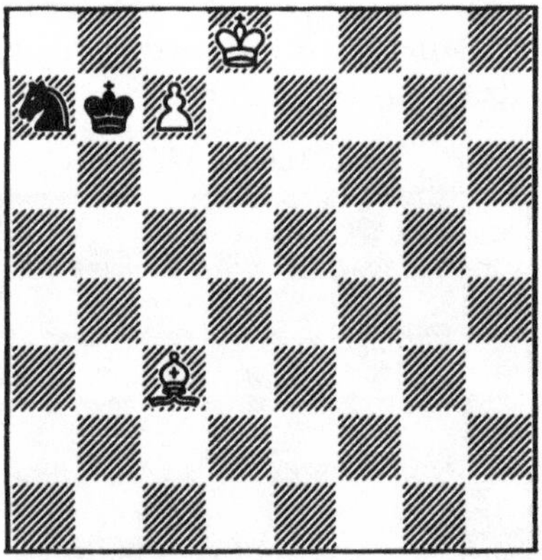

1 ♔d7 ♘c8 2 ♗d4 ♘e7 3 ♗e3 ♘c8 4 ♗c5

Up to here everything has gone

as in the previous example, but now there follows:

4 ... ♔a8!! 5 ♔c6 ♘b6!!

The knight is invulnerable, so it is a draw.

If the pawn has only reached the sixth rank, the weaker side's defensive possibilities increase.

79 **B**

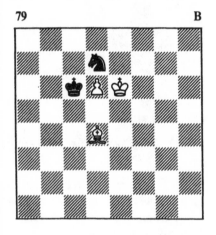

White has achieved the maximum, but he cannot completely limit the mobility of the knight; after either **1 ... ♘f8+** or **1 ... ♘b8** Black draws easily.

Proximity to the edge of the board tells unfavourably on the power of the knight, since its mobility is noticeably decreased. With a knight's pawn on the sixth rank, for example, the stronger side is able to win (see diagram 80).

After **1 ♗d7** Black immediately

80

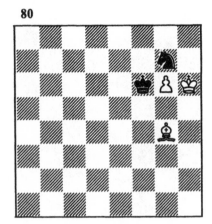

finds himself in zugzwang. If it is Black's move, however, the problem is a little more complex. In order to win White must manoeuvre to regain the move, and this is achieved as follows:

1 ... ♘e8 2 ♗d7 ♘g7 3 ♔h7 ♘h5 4 ♗g4 ♘g7 5 ♗h3 ♘h5

If 5 ... ♘e8, then 6 ♗d7 ♘g7 7 ♔h6 and wins.

6 ♔h6 ♘g7

White has attained his object, and after **7 ♗d7** it only remains for Black to lay down his arms.

We have analysed a number of positions where the square in front of the pawn was inaccessible to the bishop. Now we shall examine cases where the bishop is able to attack the square in front of the pawn.

81

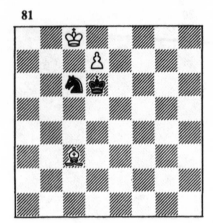

82

White's task here is to drive off the knight. If it is his move, he achieves this aim by

1 ♗b4+ ♚e6 2 ♚c7 ♚d5 3 ♗a3

Black is in zugzwang and is forced to allow the pawn to queen.

But if it is Black's move, he can save the game by improving the position of his pieces.

1 ... ♘e7+

Or 1 ... ♘a7+.

2 ♚d8 ♘c6+ 3 ♚e8 ♚e6

Black has regrouped and at the same time driven aside the white king. Now White can no longer attain a zugzwang position, so it is a draw.

If White's pawn were a rank further back, he would not succeed in winning even with the move.

Let us verify this: **1 ♗b3+ ♚e5** and then either

(i) **2 ♚c6 ♘xb3** (this is possible here) **3 d7 ♘d4+** and **4 ... ♘e6** or

(ii) **2 ♗c4 ♚d4 3 ♗f7 ♘a6+ 4 ♚c6 ♘b8+ 5 ♚c7 ♘a6+ 6 ♚b6 ♘b8**, when White cannot strengthen his position.

Thus, in the conflict of knight against bishop and pawn, the result is to a considerable extent determined by whether or not the stronger side can restrict entirely the mobility of the knight and obtain a zugzwang position. If so, then victory is achieved; if not, then in spite of the extra pawn, one must be satisfied with a draw.

In conclusion, let us examine a very old position, well known since the middle of the nineteenth century.

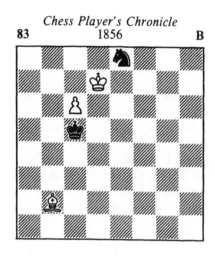

Chess Player's Chronicle
83   1856   B

White achieves a zugzwang by means of an interesting manoeuvre.

Black has only one move, **1 ... ♔b6**, for both 1 ... ♔b5 and 1 ... ♔d5 lose immediately on account of 2 ♗d4, when he is already in zugzwang.

2 ♗e5 ♔c5! 3 ♗c3 ♔b6 4 ♗a5+ ♔b5 5 ♗d8

The threat of ... ♘f6+ must be parried.

5 ... ♔c5 6 ♗h4 ♔b5 7 ♗g5!

This waiting move is decisive.

7 ... ♔c5 8 ♗e3+ ♔d5 9 ♗d4!

White has obtained the zugzwang position and wins easily after **9 ... ♘d6 10 c7.**

Knight and Pawn versus Bishop

In this ending the outcome is determined by whether one can drive off the bishop or intercept it with the knight on the diagonal on which it is operating.

84

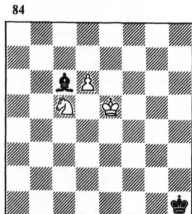

In this position the bishop copes excellently with the pawn, and it is not possible either to drive it away or intercept it. Let us check this.

1 ♔e6 ♗b5 2 ♔e7 ♗c6 3 ♔d8 ♗b5 4 ♔c7 ♔g1 5 ♘d3 ♔h1 6 ♘e5 ♗e8!

White threatened to close off the diagonal to the bishop by 7 ♘c6, so Black transfers it to another rank.

7 ♘d7 ♔g1 8 ♔d8 ♗g6 9 ♔e7 ♗f5 10 ♘c5 ♗c8!

Again Black parries the threat in time.

11 ♘d7 ♔h1 12 ♔d8 ♗a6 13

♔c7 ♗b5 14 ♘e5 ♗e8!

And White has achieved nothing.

Black prevented the opponent's pawn from queening without even bringing his king to the bishop's aid. This arose from the fact that the black bishop had not less than five squares at its disposal on the e8-a4 and c8-h3 diagonals, whilst the king and knight can only keep four under attack.

85

The above position is very interesting. In this case Black cannot do without the help of his king.

Here the bishop has four squares on the d8-a5 diagonal, of which two, d8 and a5, are taken away by the knight. If the white king gets to b7, where it attacks b6 and c7, the bishop will be unable to remain on the d8-a5 diagonal and

White will win.

Can Black counteract this in any way?

1 ♔d5 ♔a3

Had Black played 1 ... ♔b3, White would have brought into operation the other threat arising out of 1 ♔d5. After 2 ♘d4+ he would be able to cut off the bishop, for against any king move he would continue 3 ♘e6 ♗a5 4 ♔c6 and 5 ♘c7.

2 ♔c4!

A necessary finesse. The natural 2 ♔c5 is answered by 2 ... ♔a4!, and White is in zugzwang. Nor does 2 ♘d4 ♗d8! 3 ♘e6 ♗h4! promise anything, as the bishop has transferred to the longer diagonal.

2 ... ♔a4 3 ♔c5!

But now it is Black who is in zugzwang. He is compelled to retreat his king and open the way to White's. White wins after

3 ... ♔a3 4 ♔b5 ♔b2 5 ♔a6 and **6 ♔b7**.

Accordingly, if there are less than five squares on the diagonal from which the bishop keeps watch on the pawn, the participation of the king determines the result. If it can prevent the bishop from being driven off or intercepted, it is a draw; if not, then the weaker side loses.

Had it been Black's move in diagram 85, he would have had time to neutralise White's threat.

1 ... ♔b3 2 ♔d5

Or 2 ♘d4+ ♔c4.

2 ... ♔c3!

2 ... ♔a4 3 ♔c5! leads to a loss.

3 ♔c5 ♔d3 4 ♔b5 ♔e4 5 ♔a6 ♔d5 6 ♔b7 ♔d6

Black could not stop White's king from reaching b7, but he was able to bring his own to the help of the bishop. Thanks to this manoeuvre the bishop has retained its place on the d8-a5 diagonal and not allowed the enemy pawn to queen. It is therefore a draw.

With a rook's pawn the stronger side's task looks very easy. The bishop has but one diagonal at its disposal, and so it is not difficult to drive it away and cut it off – given that the opponent's king is at a sufficient distance. However, even here there are some interesting special features with which the reader will find it useful to be acquainted.

White's plan in diagram 86 is to get to b8 with his king, drive away the bishop, and then close off the diagonal by ♘b7 and queen the pawn. How can Black defend against this?

86 After B.Horwitz, 1885

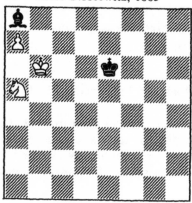

1 ♔c7 ♔e7 2 ♔c8!

The first finesse! It turns out that straightforward tactics only lead to a draw: 2 ♔b8 is followed by 2 ... ♔d8! 3 ♔xa8 (or 3 ♘b7+ ♔d7) 3 ... ♔c7!, and as we already know, White cannot win because he is unable to release his king from imprisonment. Reaching this position is Black's basic defensive resource.

2 ... ♔e8

Black at once gets into zugzwang after 2 ... ♔d6 3 ♔b8 ♔d7 4 ♘b7!, for if 4 ... ♔c6, then 5 ♔xa8 ♔c7 6 ♘d6! is decisive. In the main line too it is White's task to obtain this important zugzwang position.

3 ♘c4! ♔e7

Bishop moves lose on account of 4 ♘d6+ and 5 ♘b7.

4 ♔b8! ♔d8 5 ♘d6 ♔d7 6 ♘b7!

The zugzwang position has been achieved; Black may lay down his arms.

Rook and Pawn versus Rook

The special features of the ending of rook and pawn versus rook are graphically revealed by an analysis of the following position.

87   B

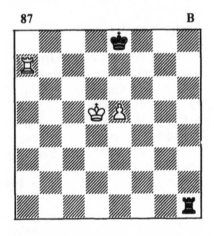

Black's king prevents the advance of the white pawn, but White is about to play 1 ♔d6 intending to drive the black king out of the way and promote the pawn – after 2 ♖a8+ ♔f7 3 e6+ ♔f6 4 ♖f8+ ♔g7 5 e7. How is Black to defend himself against this threat?

He can respond with **1 ... ♖h6**, not allowing the white king to come forward. After **2 e6** White renews the threat, trying to use the pawn as a cover.

Now passive tactics lead to defeat; **2 ... ♖g6 3 ♔d6 ♔f8 4 ♖a8+ ♔g7 5 ♔d7 ♖g1 6 e7 ♖d1+ 7 ♔c6 ♖c1+ 8 ♔d5**. The king makes for Black's rook, and the 'spite' checks quickly come to an end.

Only by immediately going over to a counter-attack by **2 ... ♖h1!** is Black able to save the game. After that White cannot strengthen the position of his pieces. Thus, **3 ♔d6** is followed by **3 ... ♖d1+**, attacking the king from behind.

4 ♔e5 ♖e1+ 5 ♔f6 ♖f1+

There is nowhere for White's king to hide from the persecution of the tiresome black rook.

The method of defence consists, therefore, in deploying the king in front of the pawn while using the rook to prevent the opponent's king from coming through ahead of the pawn. Then, when the pawn moves further forward, the rook is transferred to a new position and attacks the king from the rear. This method, which was discovered in the eighteenth century by Philidor, is fundamental to these endings.

Here is another interesting old position:

88 After A.Salvio, 1634

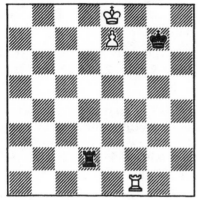

As the defending side's king is not directly stopping the pawn, the main onus of defence lies on the rook, which tries to prevent the enemy king from getting out of the way of the pawn.

After **1 ♖g1+ ♔h7** an immediate attempt by White to break free with his king is not successful. For example, **2 ♔f7 ♖f2+ 3 ♔e6 ♖e2+ 4 ♔d6 ♖d2+ 5 ♔c7 ♖e2 6 ♔d8 ♖d2+ 7 ♔e8**. In order not to lose his pawn White is obliged to bring the king back to its former place.

He ought first to have prepared the king's exit, and this object is served by

2 ♖g4!

White deploys his rook in such a way that when his king comes out into the open it will provide a defence against the checks on the file.

2 ... ♖d1 3 ♔f7 ♖f1+ 4 ♔e6 ♖e1+ 5 ♔f6 ♖f1+ 6 ♔e5 ♖e1+ 7 ♖e4

This manoeuvre is called "bridge building".

White also had another way of winning. He could have driven the enemy rook from the d-file, thus opening up a route for his king. This is accomplished as follows:

1 ♖c1 ♖d3 2 ♖c8 ♖d1 3 ♖d8! ♖e8 4 ♔d7 ♖d1+ 5 ♔c6 ♖c1+ 6 ♔d5

And the pawn queens.

Let us now return to the position in diagram 87 and suppose that Black had not found 1 ... ♖h6 but had played **1 ... ♖e1**, waiting to see how things would develop. In that case White can drive the enemy king out of the way of the pawn, commencing with

2 ♔e6

This threatens mate, so Black is forced to run with his king. First, let us presume that it goes to the right and consider what it leads to.

2 ... ♔f8 3 ♖a8+ ♔g7 4 ♖e8

After **4 ♔d6 ♔f7!** White has not improved his position, for he would still be unable to advance the pawn. His last move seems incomprehensible as yet. In order to understand what White is threatening, we shall suppose that Black remains passive: 4 ... ♖e2 5 ♔d7 ♖e1 6 e6 ♖e2 7 ♖a8. The threat is now 8 e7, so Black cannot stay passive any longer. But it is too late, as after 7 ... ♖d2+ 8 ♔e8 ♖d1 9 e7 ♖d2 a position arises which we have already studied, where White frees his king and wins by 10 ♖d8.

How then is Black to contend with White's plan? It is clear that after 4 ♖e8 the rook does not help the king to shelter from checks. Black can exploit this and play 4 ... ♖a1, immediately threatening to attack the opponent's king from the flank. Then if White replies 5 ♖d8, in order to cover himself against the checks with the rook, Black can return his rook to its former place. If White persists in carrying on with his plan and plays 5 ♔d7, then Black can put his threat into full effect: 5 ... ♖a7+ 6 ♔d6 ♖a6+ 7 ♔c7 ♔f7, with a clear draw.

Provided, therefore, that the opponent defends correctly, White is unable to strengthen his position.

It is worth noting that Black need be in no hurry with the flank attack. 4 ... ♖e2 5 ♔d7 ♖e1, awaiting developments, does not lose either. Only after 6 e6, when the pawn has moved forward and

become more dangerous, does the one road to safety consist in the rook attack from the flank. For example:

6 ... ♖a1! 7 ♖d8 ♖a7+ 8 ♔d6 ♖a6+ 9 ♔e7 ♖a7+ 10 ♖d7 ♖a8 11 ♖d8

If White manoeuvres his rook on the seventh rank, it is sufficient for a draw for Black to 'mark time' with his king on the squares g7 and g6.

11 ... ♖a7+ 12 ♔d6 ♖a6+ 13 ♔e5 ♖a5+ 14 ♖d5 ♖a1 15 ♔d6 ♔f8 and draws.

The rook attack from the flank is an important defensive device in these endings. In fact, when the pawn is far advanced and the opposing king is not in its path, the draw – if it is at all possible – is generally achieved by means of the rook attack from the flank.

Now we shall try to define in what cases the flank attack does not succeed. Let us go back again to the position shown in diagram 87 and after 1 ... ♖e1 2 ♔e6 play, instead of 2 ... ♔f8, 2 ... ♔d8. There may then follow 3 ♖a8+ ♔c7 4 ♖e8.

(see diagram 89)

Now – and this is very important – Black has only one possible way of saving the game. That is, an immediate rook attack from the flank.

89   B

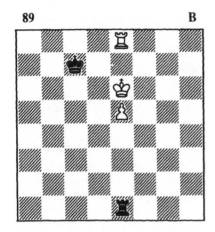

4 ... 🖢h1! 5 🖢g8 🖢e1!

Black must play accurately; he loses after 5 ... 🖢h6+ 6 ♔f7 🖢h7+ 7 ♔f6 🖢h6+ 8 🖢g6 🖢h8 9 ♔f7.

6 🖢g2 ♔d8, with a draw.

It required but a slight delay on Black's part and White would have won. For example:

4 ... 🖢e2? 5 ♔f7 🖢h2

Black has lost one tempo and the flank attack is too late.

6 🖢g8!

6 e6? 🖢h7+ 7 ♔g6 🖢h1! leads only to a draw.

6 ... 🖢h7+ 7 🖢g7 🖢h8 8 ♔e7 ♔c6 9 e6 ♔c7

It turns out now that the rook does not have enough space for the flank attack, so Black is ruined.

10 🖢g1 🖢h7+ 11 ♔f6 🖢h6+ 12 ♔f7 🖢h7+ 13 ♔g6 🖢h2

Or 13 ... 🖢e7 14 ♔f6.

14 🖢d1! 🖢e2 15 ♔f7 🖢h2

As a rule, for the rook attack from the flank to be successful when the pawn is far advanced the rook must be at a distance of at least three squares from the pawn. Here this distance equals two squares, and the flank attack therefore proves ineffective.

16 e7 🖢h7+ 17 ♔f6 🖢h6+ 18 ♔g7 🖢e6 19 ♔f7, and White wins.

However, if we examine the situation after White's 14th move but transferred a file to the left, it will be found that in this position, where the rook has more room for the flank attack, Black possesses sufficient resources to save the game.

90   B

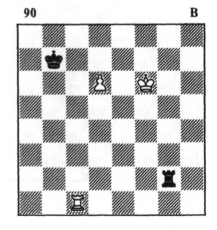

Here 1 ... ♖d2 2 ♔e7 ♖h2! leads to a draw, as the following variations show:

3 d7 ♖h7+ 4 ♔e6 ♖h6+ 5 ♔e5

Or 5 ♔f7 ♖h7+ 6 ♔e8 ♖h8+.

5 ... ♖h5+ 6 ♔f6 ♖h6+ 7 ♔f5 ♖d6

Nor does an attempt to bring the rook up to the help of the king improve the situation. Black answers 3 ♖f1 by 3 ... ♔c6 4 ♖f6 ♖h7+ 5 ♔d8 ♖h8+ 6 ♔e7 ♖h7+ 7 ♔e6 ♖d7 8 ♔e5 ♖h7 with a clear draw.

Yet another system of defence, which may be called rook attack from the front, is possible in positions where the pawn has not advanced far. The essence of this method of defence is seen from the following example.

91

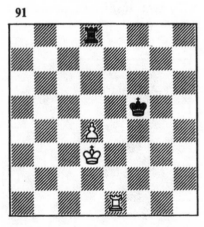

Black's king is cut off from the pawn, but thanks to the favourable position of his rook it is not possible for White to advance the pawn.

Let us verify this.

1 ♔c4 ♖c8+ 2 ♔b5 ♖d8 3 ♔c5 ♖c8+ 4 ♔b6 ♖d8!

Checking with the rook (4 ... ♖b8+) would be fatal for Black, as after 5 ♔c7 the pawn cannot be stopped; whilst the flank attack does not yield results here on account of the lack of space for the rook to operate in.

5 ♔c5

Or 5 ♖d1 ♔e6.

5 ... ♖c8+ 6 ♔b4 ♖d8 7 ♔c4 ♖c8+ 8 ♔d3 ♖d8

Owing to Black's active defence White is unable to strengthen his position.

In the example that we have just examined the attack from the front proved effective because the distance between the rook and the pawn was not less than three squares.

At first glance it may seem that the black king does not assist the rook during a frontal attack. However, that is not so. Were the king on a less favourable square, say f7, then White, with the move, would win.

92

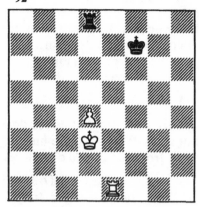

1 ♔c4 ♖c8+ 2 ♔b5 ♖d8 3 ♔c5 ♖c8+ 4 ♔b6 ♖d8 5 ♖e4!

This is the whole point. White has acquired the possibility of defending the pawn with his rook, whereas before the enemy king prevented it. Now White can strengthen his position.

5 ... ♔f6 6 ♔c7 ♖d5

Or 6 ... ♔f5 7 ♖e5+.

7 ♔c6 ♖d8 8 d5

And the pawn queens.

On the other hand, if it is Black's turn to move, he obtains a draw – and in two ways even.

1 ... ♖e8!

The simplest.

2 ♖xe8

If White's rook leaves the e-file, the black king will assume a

position in front of the pawn.

2 ... ♔xe8 3 ♔c4

The struggle has come down to a pawn ending, and in such endings the fight for key squares acquires great significance. Black saves the game if he prevents the white king from reaching the key squares (in relation to the d-pawn) c6, d6 and e6.

From c4 White's king can reach d5 and c5. Black must have his king on d7 when White's is on d5; on c7 when it is on c5. Black's king reaches these squares from d8, so he is obliged to reply 3 ... ♔d8!.

1 ... ♔f6, improving the position of the king, also leads to a draw. For example:

2 ♔c4 ♖c8+ 3 ♔b5 ♖d8 4 ♔c5 ♖c8+ 5 ♔b6 ♖d8! 6 ♖e4 ♔f5 7 ♖h4 ♔e6

with a draw, since White is again unable to advance the pawn.

We shall now examine how the promotion of a rook's pawn is achieved. Here the chances of winning are, as a rule, less than with other pawns. The king can support a rook's pawn from but one side, while the pawn only defends the king against checks from the rear. If the weaker side's king is in front of the pawn, then one may confidently say that the ending will finish as a draw.

93

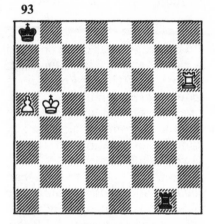

Black's defence is very simple. If 1 ♔b6, for example, it is enough to guard against the mate by 1 ... ♖g8 and then to move the rook along the back rank. White has no way whatsoever of strengthening his position.

Even when the weaker side's king does not stop the pawn directly there are still many possibilities of saving the game.

94

In a similar position with any other pawn White wins easily by bringing his king out into the open. With a rook's pawn it is not possible to free the king.

For example:

1 ♖h2 ♖c1

This is the simplest. Black does not allow White to drive his king away from the c8 and c7 squares.

1 ... ♖b3 2 ♖c2+ ♔d7 3 ♖c1 ♖b2! does not lose either. In spite of the fact that Black's king has been driven two files from the pawn, the white king cannot escape from its imprisonment. It is interesting that Black's drawing chances here are so great that he may even let the white king out of its cage in certain cases. Thus, instead of 2 ... ♔d7, it also proves possible to play **2 ... ♔d6**, allowing White's rook to reach the eighth rank. True, Black must thereafter defend accurately: after **3 ♖c8** the only way to draw here is to retire the rook along the third rank, for example:

3 ... ♖a3

The king then emerges from shelter but immediately comes under fire from Black's rook.

4 ♔b7 ♖b3+ 5 ♔a6 ♖a3+ 6 ♔b6 ♖b3+ 7 ♔a5 ♖a3+

and it is clear that the king cannot break away from the pawn. If

White tries to prepare the king's exit and plays 4 ♖b8, then after 4 ... ♔c7 he, alas, loses the chance. The withdrawal of the rook from the b-file was the only way to save the game. After 3 ... ♔d7? 4 ♖b8! ♖c3 5 ♔b7 ♖b3+ 6 ♔a6 ♖a3+ 7 ♔b6 ♖b3+ 8 ♔c5 the white king is liberated and victory achieved.

In order to establish how many squares the black king can be cut off from the pawn without the risk of losing, let us examine the following position.

95

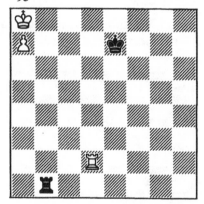

It turns out that here too, given correct defence by Black, the king is unable to break free: for while White is transferring his rook to b8 Black has time to reach c7 with his king. So the king replaces the rook in the role of a guard. For example:

1 ♖h2 ♔d7! 2 ♖h8 ♔c7.

Only when the king is cut off four files from the pawn is White able to win.

96

1 ♖c2 ♔e7 2 ♖c8 ♔d7

The black king is late arriving at the 'prison gates', and so White wins after

3 ♖b8 ♖a1 4 ♔b7

We shall now investigate positions where the weaker side's rook occupies the square in front of the pawn. In such cases the result generally depends on which king is the quicker to get to the pawn.

(see diagram 97)

If it is his move here, White comes first in the king race, for example **1 ♔d6 ♔b5 2 ♔c7** and **3 ♔b7**, winning easily.

On the other hand, if you begin to analyse the above position with

97   G.Zeibot, 1899

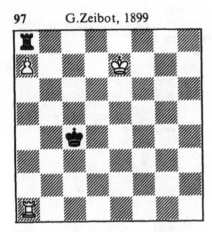

Black to move, then it seems that after 1 ... ♔b5 2 ♔d6 ♔b6 Black saves himself by liquidating his main enemy – the passed pawn. However, there follows 3 ♖b1+ ♔xa7 4 ♔c7, and Black falls out of the frying-pan into the fire: in view of the threat of mate he is obliged to give up his rook. Nor does refusing to take the pawn at once improve matters. 3 ... ♔a6 is answered by 4 ♔c7! ♖xa7+ (now capturing is forced) 5 ♔c6, and Black is again in a hopeless position.

The correct continuation is the far from obvious move:

1 ... ♔c5!

Black approaches the pawn, at the same time 'shouldering' the white king aside and preventing it from occupying the important d6 square.

2 ♔d7 ♔b6 3 ♖b1+ ♔c5!

Black defends with precision and prudently declines the "Greek gift".

4 ♖b7 ♖h8!

Another fine move! Black makes use of the poor position of the white pieces and activates his rook.

5 ♔c7

If 5 ♖b8, then 5 ... ♖h7+ and 6 ... ♖xa7.

5 ... ♖a8

And White cannot strengthen his position. It is a draw.

98

From the point of view of exploiting the extra pawn, Position No. 98, in which the rook defends the pawn from the promoting square, is less happy. In this case a draw is possible even though the weaker side's king is at a great distance from the pawn.

In order to achieve this victory it is necessary for White to free his rook. But this cannot be done, since on **1 ♔b6** Black starts worrying the white king by checking it from behind until it leaves the pawn. Then the black rook attacks the pawn from the rear again and does not allow White's rook to free itself. Moreover, Black's king must not interfere in the play; it should manoeuvre on the squares g7 and h7. Any attempt to approach with the king will backfire fatally: 1 ... ♔f7 2 ♖h8! ♖xa7 3 ♖h7+ and 4 ♖xa7.

There is another interesting method of defence which is undoubtedly useful for the reader to know.

99 J.Berger, 1922

In order to win in the above position it is enough for White to break free with his rook with check. But this cannot be accomplished, since all the time the king hides "in the shadow" of the opponent's king.

For example:

1 ♔f7 ♔f5! 2 ♔e7 ♔e5! 3 ♔d7 ♔d5 4 ♔c7 ♔c5 5 ♔b7

The pawn sacrifice 5 ♖c8 ♖xa7+ 6 ♔b8+ does not succeed, as there is the reply 6 ... ♔b6.

5 ... ♖b1+

However, if Black were to quit the fifth rank with his king, it would lead to his defeat: 1 ... ♔f4? 2 ♔e6 ♔e4 3 ♔d6 ♔d4 4 ♔c6 ♔c4 5 ♖c8! (now this is possible) 5 ... ♖xa7 6 ♔b6+, and White wins the rook.

And here is one more curious position, where Black saves the game by hiding his king in the 'shadow' of his own rook.

100 **B**

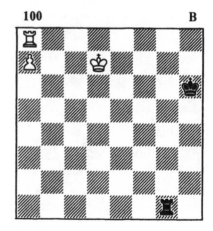

1 ... ☖g7+ 2 ☗c6 ☗g5!

In stepping into the "shadow", the king leaves the g6 square free for the rook so that it can use the sixth rank to harass the opponent's king.

3 ☗b6 ☖g6+ 4 ☗b5 ☖g7 5 ☗a5 ☗g4 Drawn

White is unable to improve his position.

We have examined a number of examples where the white king was able to approach the pawn without difficulty but had nowhere to hide from the persecution of the annoying black rook.

If the pawn is on the sixth rank, White's king has the chance to take refuge behind the pawn when checked from the rear. In that case the essential factor is whether or not it will later be able to leave its shelter.

101

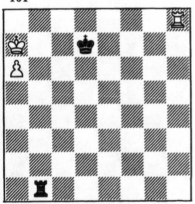

Here the white king is unable to free itself. For example:

1 ☖b8 ☖a1 2 ☗b7 ☖b1+ 3 ☗a8 ☖a1 4 a7 ☗c7

Black would also not have lost with his king on d6, although there it finds itself less favourably placed.

102

1 ☖b8 ☖a1 2 ☗b7 ☖b1+ 3 ☗c8 ☖c1+!

3 ... ☖a1 4 ☖b6+ ☗c5 5 ☗b7 ☖h1 6 ☖c6+ ☗b5 7 a7 leads to defeat.

4 ☗d8 ☖h1!

The poor placing of White's pieces permits the black rook to occupy a more active position.

5 ☖b6+ ☗c5 6 ☖e6 ☖h8+ 7 ☗d7 ☖h7+

In conclusion, here is one more important position.

103 After J.Vanchura, 1924

White cannot achieve any success here, since the beautifully placed black rook easily parries all the threats.

For example:

1 ♔b5 ♖f5+ 2 ♔c4 ♖f6!

He must not be tempted by checks.

3 ♔d5 ♖b6 4 ♔e5 ♖c6 5 a7 ♖a6! Drawn

The white king was unable to reach the refuge at a7.

Queen and Pawn versus Queen

If the weaker side's king is in the path of the pawn and his queen can obstruct the attack of the opponent's pieces, a draw is a perfectly natural result. When defending against checks, the stronger side's king will have to be covered by the queen, and that will lead to a drawn king and pawn ending. The positions which afford interest here are those where the weaker side's king is unable to participate in the struggle with the pawn and so his task is laid upon the queen alone.

104

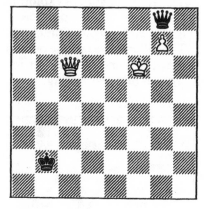

Black's queen prevents the advance of the pawn but occupies a passive position. In order to win it is necessary for White to drive it away from g8, and this needs to be done accurately so as to avert perpetual check. There are two lines that lead to victory:

a) **1 ♕b5+ ♔a2 2 ♕a4+ ♔b2 3 ♕b4+ ♔a1 4 ♕f8 ♕b3**. The queen is forced to leave g8, but Black does not yet lose hope of perpetual check. **5 g8=♕ ♕f3+ 6 ♔g7 ♕g4+ 7 ♔h8 ♕h5+ 8 ♕h7** and Black may resign.

b) 1 ♕e6 ♕d8+ 2 ♔g6! ♕d3+ 3 ♔f7! ♔c1 4 g8=♕ ♕f3+ 5 ♔g7 ♕g2+ 6 ♔h7 ♕b7+ 7 ♕g7 ♕b1+ 8 ♕eg6, and the checks are finished.

The method of defence against checks that White employed is typical of these endings. White manoeuvres his king in such a way as to make sure of exploiting the position of the opponent's king for defence against the checks.

The following example demonstrates the same device, but in a more complicated setting.

105   B

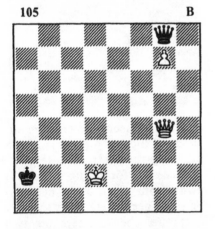

It would appear that the white king has nowhere to hide and that Black can start pursuing it with endless checks. In fact, the king escapes from the checks comparatively quickly, and White queens the pawn. For example:

1 ... ♕d5+ 2 ♔e1!

Accuracy is required. After the incautious 2 ♔e2 ♕b5+!, to escape from perpetual check White would have had to embark on a long journey with his king to h8, but this would not have won him the game.

2 ... ♕h1+

2 ... ♕a5+ is followed by 3 ♔f1!, and the checks are at an end.

3 ♔f2 ♕h2+ 4 ♕g2

Having set an ambush with his queen, White immediately decides the game in his favour. 4 ... ♕h4+ is answered by 5 ♔f3+ and 6 g8=♕.

It remains to be added that if Black continues to stand his ground passively, leaving his queen on g8, White is not at all obliged to advance his king towards the pawn; he first moves it away into 'hiding' at g1; then, by checking, he gets his queen to f8 with tempo and drives off the black queen; finally, he queens the pawn.

Unlike other pieces, a queen on its own, without the help of the king, can assure the promotion of a pawn. This is a very important characteristic of queen and pawn endings.

We shall now examine a case where the queen prevents the advance of the pawn by pinning it on the rank.

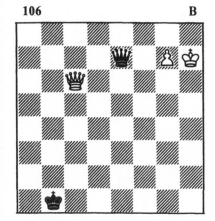

106 B

Here, too, White is successful and can free himself from the pin. And as before, to White's aid comes . . . the enemy king. 1 ♔g6 is threatened, so Black must check:

1 ... ♛h4+ 2 ♛h6 ♛e7 3 ♛b6+

In order to win White must occupy one of four squares (c6, d5, d4 or f4) with check. Thus, if 3 ... ♔a1, then 4 ♛d4+ ♔b1 5 ♔h8 is immediately decisive, while if 3 ... ♔c2, then 4 ♛c6+ ♔b1 5 ♔g6.

The most tenacious reply is 3 ... ♔a2, but even then after 4 ♛a5+ ♔b1 5 ♛b5+ ♔a1 6 ♛a4+ ♔b1 7 ♛d1+ the queen reaches either d4 or d5 with gain of tempo.

If the weaker side's king is unable to take part in the struggle against the pawn in this type of ending, it must try to get as far away from it as possible, lest the opponent exploit its position to execute the winning manoeuvre.

The strongest weapon of defence in this ending is the pin on the diagonal, but the bad placing of the king may still permit the opponent to free himself from the pin. Here is an example on this theme:

107

1 ♔h7 ♛h1+

The pin on the rank is of no help, e.g. 1 ... ♛d7 2 ♛e4+! ♔a3 3 ♔g8, and the pawn queens.

2 ♔g7! ♛a1+

Or 2 ... ♛b7 3 ♛b1+.

3 ♔g8 ♛a2 4 ♛c6!

An interesting position! Black is unexpectedly found to be in zugzwang, not having a single good move. The reader may

satisfy himself of this.
If the position of the opponent's king cannot be exploited for the purpose of defending against perpetual check, then the ending should end in a draw.

5 Practical Endings

After the reader has conscientiously studied the first four chapters the designation "beginner" will no longer, it seems to me, be quite appropriate, for he should know how to find his bearings in the endgame. However, elementary knowledge is still not enough to enable one to handle the endgame with understanding.

It is not enough to know that an extra pawn is an important advantage in an ending and that to win the game it is necessary to queen this pawn. What is very important is to be able to accomplish this in practice.

The time has come to try to acquaint the reader with the various processes typical of play in the endgame. It is not at all necessary to remember these positions. The important thing is to master the methods of attack and defence and to understand the general plan.

When examining positions one must pay chief attention, not to a detailed analysis of variations, but to appraising the position, identifying an advantage, forming a plan to exploit it, and to the tactical features occurring during the execution of this plan.

We shall begin with an examination of endings where, apart from the kings, only pawns remain on the board. These are called pawn endings.

Pawn Endings

First, let us acquaint ourselves with the classification of pawns.

108

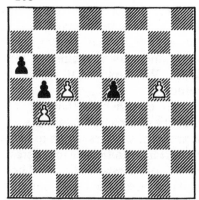

The pawns at b4 and b5 – the characteristic feature of their state

73

is that they are, as it were, in 'head-on opposition' to each other – are called blocked pawns.

The pawns at c5, e5 and g5 are called passed pawns, since there are no enemy pawns in their way. Passed pawns also have their distinctions. The c-pawn is a protected passed pawn, while the e- and g-pawns are isolated. Moreover, the g-pawn, the most distant from the main mass of pawns, is an outside passed pawn.

The theory of pawn endings has been worked out considerably more fully than the others. However, owing to the fact that the questions involved have long been studied aside from practice, many conclusions which have a practical significance have remained largely unknown. But they can undoubtedly facilitate the understanding and handling of pawn endings.

Certain interesting conclusions have already been made during our examination of endings with king and pawn against a lone king. We now recall these to mind.

We established that in the vicinity of a passed pawn there is a group of squares which have an important significance in the treatment of these endings. These squares are called key squares, since the occupation of one of them by the stronger side's king means the realisation of the object

of the ending – the pawn goes irresistibly on to queen. Here the play consists basically in the king's fight for the key squares. The side that has the pawn strives to penetrate with the king to one of the key squares, while the opponent tries to prevent it.

The conception of key squares can be extended to other pawn configurations as well. Here is an example.

109

We have before us a very simple position with blocked pawns. White's plan in this position falls into two stages. He must first win the opponent's pawn and then queen his own. It is clear that if the white king is able to occupy one of the following six squares, e5, f5, g5, a5, b5 or c5, the fall of the black d-pawn is inevitable. Consequently, these squares may also with every right be called key squares, for their occupation by the stronger side's king (in this case White's) leads to the fulfilment of the immediate objective – winning the pawn.

It follows that a blocked pawn has its own system of key squares. We should observe that the attainment of the first objective (winning the pawn) says nothing yet about achieving the second (promoting the pawn). Having suffered a reverse in the struggle for the pawn and lost it, the weaker side may be able to prevent the opponent from queening his pawn. And it is this phenomenon that we find here. If it is his move, Black is forced to allow the opponent's king to reach his pawn's key squares. Thus, **1 ... ♚e6** is followed by **2 ♔g5 ♚e7 3 ♔f5 ♚d6 4 ♔f6 ♚c6 5 ♔e5**, and Black loses his pawn. However, he then plays **5 ... ♚c7! 6 ♔xd5 ♚d7!** and draws the game: White's king does not reach the key squares of the passed d-pawn.

A legitimate question may occur to the reader: "But what is the practical advantage to be gained from introducing the conception of key squares?"

In the next example we shall show that this conception facilitates the analysis of a whole series of pawn endings, enabling one to establish a clear plan of play quickly and unerringly.

110 N.Grigoriev, 1921 **B**

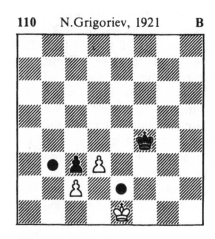

White threatens to win the game at once by playing ♔e2. After that he will be able to drive the king back, mobilise his d-pawn, and win Black's only pawn. It is not difficult to perceive that e2 will be the first key square. It is also easy to find a second – b3. Having reached that too, White wins the pawn. Black draws if he can prevent the opponent's king getting to one of the key squares. This is only possible with **1 ... ♚f3!** For example **2 ♔d1 ♚e3 3 ♔c1 ♚d4 4 ♔b1 ♚c5 5 ♔a2 ♚b4!**, and the black king has arrived in time. It is easy to check for oneself that **1 ... ♚e3** leads to a loss.

If, after **1 ... ♚f3**, White tries to go round to the right with his king, Black aims for the c-pawn, wins it, and queens his own pawn. The reader is again left to satisfy himself on this point.

When the white king moves from e1 to a2 the black king has but one way of getting from f3 to b4 in time to prevent White from seizing the key square b3. The kings' routes are, as it were, mutually connected. For each move of the white king's the black king has just one reply. f3 corresponds only to e1; e3 to d1; d4 to c1; c5 to b1; b4 to a2. Such a mutual connection between squares is called "correspondence", and the squares themselves have received the designation "corresponding squares". Corresponding squares, by way of being the signposts of the king's road, are the lighthouses in the limitless sea of variations. The black king, in order to stop White's from gaining control of the key squares, must proceed via the corresponding squares and no others. Thus, the correspondence of squares represents for the kings a means of contesting the key squares.

In the example given the black king was able to maintain the correspondence, and the ending was a draw. Such a favourable outcome for the weaker side occurs far from always. In the following example we shall show that if the correspondence cannot be maintained, defeat is inevitable.

At first glance it seems that Black can defend himself successfully here. If 1 ♔c5, threatening to

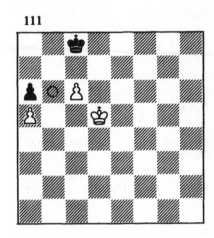

111

penetrate to the key square b6, Black has the single but sufficient reply 1 ... ♔c7, while if 1 ♔d6, he has 1 ... ♔d8. Again we have a case of corresponding squares. c7 corresponds to c5; d8 to d6; c8 to d5. Therefore, Black is able to maintain the correspondence of squares close to the pawn. Let us try retreating the king – say, 1 ♔d4. Will Black then be able to find a corresponding square for his king? Obviously, Black cannot reply 1 ... ♔c7, as White's king breaks through to b6 after 2 ♔c5! that means Black must play either 1 ... ♔d8 or 1 ... ♔b8. But if we make another waiting move – 2 ♔c4 – what then? It is not hard to satisfy oneself that the balance cannot be preserved in that case. After 2 ... ♔c8 (if 2 ... ♔c7 then 3 ♔c5, and the king penetrates to b6) there follows 3 ♔d5! ♔d8 4 ♔d6 ♔c8

5 c7.

We have examined one of the simplest cases of the application of corresponding squares, the so-called "triangulation". By manoeuvring his king in a triangle (the d5, d4 and c4 squares) White succeeds in disturbing the correspondence in his favour. In order to make two steps forward the white king takes a step back.

The ability to make use of the laws of corresponding squares is of great significance in the analysis of many positions with blocked pawns. As we shall see further on, corresponding squares do not only exist in pawn endings. Indeed, one may speak of corresponding squares in any position where it is necessary to look for a uniquely correct reply. And in every case the corresponding squares prove important reference points, noticeably facilitating analysis.

112   I.Maizelis, 1921

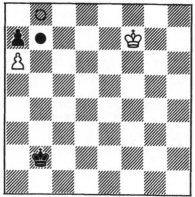

We shall now consider certain characteristic features of the geometry of the chessboard.

White wins the pawn if it is his move. For Black to save the game, his king must succeed in reaching c7 the moment White takes the pawn. Then the white king will be unable to gain control of either of the key squares (b7 or b8) and so the draw will be secured.

The white king can approach the enemy pawn by various routes in the same number of moves, e.g., ♔e7-d7-c7-b7-a7 or ♔e6-d6-c6-b7-a7 or ♔e6-d5-c6-b7-a7. Even the following route is possible: ♔e8-d7-c8-b7-a7.

Is this not a surprising thing? Ever since our school days we have known that the shortest distance between two points is a straight line and that the route that takes the straight line is always shorter than the indirect one. But on the chessboard, as we see, it is not always like that. Here the direct and indirect routes are equal!

The valid question then arises: could not the white king both move towards the pawn and at the same time obstruct the progress of Black's king to c7? It turns out that such a combination of tasks can be carried out.

By continuing **1 ♔e6 ♔c3 2 ♔d5!**, the white king, as it were, 'shoulders off' the black king. The latter is forced to give way and can no longer get through in time, for example, 2 ... ♔b4 3 ♔c6 ♔a5 4 ♔b7 ♔b5 5 ♔xa7 ♔c6 6 ♔b8, and White wins.

But for the rarest exceptions, one extra pawn is enough for victory in pawn endings. Converting this advantage into a win does not present great difficulties. One must create a passed pawn and queen it. If the opponent's king succeeds in preventing the pawn from queening, then, by exploiting its deflection, the stronger side's king breaks through to the enemy pawns and gains a decisive material advantage.

Before creating a passed pawn, one is usually advised to improve the position of one's king. The purpose of this is to be able to advance the pawn with the greatest possible effect and without

113

allowing the opponent any chances. As an example of how to exploit a passed pawn, let us examine diagram 113.

1 ♔f1

The king needs to be brought into play.

1 ... ♔e7 2 ♔e2 ♔d6 3 b4

Also possible is 3 ♔d3 ♔c5 4 ♔c3 and then 5 b4.

3 ... ♔d5 4 ♔d3 f5 5 f4 g6 6 g3 a6 7 a4 ♔c6

The king is unable to remain in an active position; it is running out of moves and must retire.

8 ♔d4 ♔d6 9 b5 axb5 10 axb5 ♔c7 11 ♔e5

This is the simplest. White gives up his passed pawn but obtains a decisive material superiority on the other wing. Also possible was 11 ♔c5 ♔b7 12 b6 ♔b8 13 ♔c6 ♔c8 14 b7+ ♔b8 15 ♔b6 h6 (or 15 ... h5 16 ♔c6) 16 h4 g5 (a desperate attempt to play for stalemate) 17 hxg5 hxg5 18 fxg5 f4 19 g6 f3 20 g7 f2 21 g8=♕ mate.

11 ... ♔b6 12 ♔f6 ♔xb5 13 ♔g7 ♔c4 14 ♔xh7 ♔d4 15 ♔xg6, and White wins.

The reader should note the straightforward manner in which White conducted his winning plan. Of course, this example was to a large extent ideal, but we can say with confidence that in the majority of cases converting a material advantage into a win in a pawn ending is accomplished without great difficulty.

In the following examples we shall take a look at the special features of pawn endings with equal material.

114

In this position the distant location of the black king enables White to effect an important tactical device – a pawn breakthrough. After **1 b6! cxb6 2 a6!! bxa6 3 c6** the c-pawn queens. If Black had played **1 ... axb6**, a symmetrical variation would have occurred: **2 c6!! bxc6 3 a6**, and it is the a-pawn which queens.

One must always reckon with the possibility of a pawn breakthrough.

Now here is a position illustra-

ting a more favourable pawn formation.

115

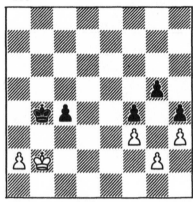

The outside passed pawn – White's a-pawn – is much more dangerous than the black c-pawn. White exchanges these pawns, after which his king is left much nearer to the opposing pawns and he obtains a decisive material superiority.

1 ⌘c2 ⌘a3

If Black is obstinate about exchanging pawns and continues 1 ... ⌘c5 then after 2 ⌘c3 ⌘b5 3 a3 ⌘c5 4 a4 ⌘d5 5 a5 ⌘c5 6 a6 the exchange is forced in even more unfavourable circumstances.

2 ⌘c3 ⌘xa2 3 ⌘xc4 ⌘b2 4 ⌘d4 ⌘c2 5 ⌘e4 ⌘d2 6 ⌘f5 ⌘e2 7 ⌘xg5 ⌘f2 8 ⌘xf4 ⌘xg2 9 ⌘g4, and White wins.

In this case the black king was

far too 'late for the train', but sometimes even one tempo may be significant. Here is a typical example:

116

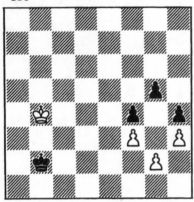

Both kings are bent on attacking the opponent's pawns, but it is White's turn to move and that is decisive.

1 ♔c4 ♔c2 2 ♔d4 ♔d2 3 ♔e4 ♔e2 4 ♔f5 ♔f2 5 ♔xg5 ♔xg2

It would seem that the annihilation of the pawns must have a peaceful outcome, but there follows:

6 ♔g4!

and wherever Black moves, he loses. For example:

6 ... ♔f2 7 ♔xf4 or 6 ... ♔h2 7 ♔xh4

We conclude our examination of pawn endings with the following example.

117   **B**

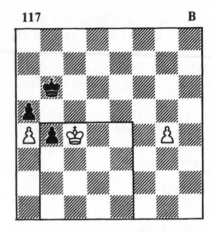

Black has a protected passed pawn; that is a big advantage, since his king is free and can set off towards White's passed pawn. Meanwhile, White's king must remain in the square of the black b-pawn. Let us consider a possible continuation.

1 ... ♔c6 2 ♔d4 ♔d6 3 ♔e4 ♔e6 4 ♔e3 ♔f6 5 ♔d4 ♔g5 6 ♔e3 ♔xg4 7 ♔e4!

Black has won the pawn, but the struggle is not yet over. White tries to organise a defence.

7 ... ♔g5

7 ... ♔g3 8 ♔e3! ♔g2 9 ♔e2! would be futile, as the black king cannot get through.

8 ♔e3 ♔f5 9 ♔d3 ♔e5 10 ♔d2 ♔d4 11 ♔c2 ♔c4 12 ♔b2! ♔d4

Black sees through the cunning trap: the attempt to decide the game at once by 12 ... b3? leads to stalemate after 13 ♔a3! ♔c3. To achieve victory Black must win the a-pawn, but he has to take a long, roundabout route to get at it.

13 ♔c2 ♔e3 14 ♔c1 ♔d3 15 ♔b2 ♔d2! 16 ♔b3 ♔c1! 17 ♔a2 ♔c2 18 ♔a1 ♔b3!

It was still not too late to make a mistake: 18 ... b3?? gave stalemate.

19 ♔b1 ♔xa4, and Black wins.

Knight Endings

With a large number of pawns on the board, converting an extra pawn into a win may not, as a rule, be much more complicated in a knight ending than in a pawn ending. In its most general features the method of winning is the same: after improving the position of one's pieces (here king, knight and pawns) one creates a passed pawn and strives to queen it. Beyond that it depends on the defensive plan. If the opponent's knight tries to block the passed pawn by itself, then one must drive it away. While if the king goes to the aid of the knight, it is usually possible to exploit the diversion of forces and obtain a decisive material advantage by forcing one's way through with either king or knight to the opponent's pawns on the other wing.

Here is an example that corresponds to No. 113.

118

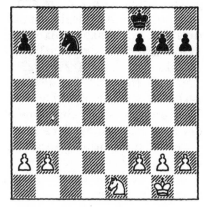

At first White improves the position of his king by moving it over to the queenside, where it will later be necessary to create a passed pawn.

1 ♔f1 ♔e7 2 ♔e2 ♔d6 3 ♔d3 ♔c5

Naturally, Black wishes to make use of the slightly more active position of his king to hinder his opponent from creating a passed pawn.

4 ♘c2 ♘d5 5 g3

One must be careful. Black was threatening to win a pawn by 5 ... ♘f4+.

5 ... a5 6 b3 f5 7 a3 g6 8 b4+!

It looked as if Black had prevented a passed pawn from being created, but after this powerful move his hopes go up in smoke. White sacrifices his extra pawn in order to transpose into a pawn ending with a more active king position. A typical variation runs: 8 ... axb4 9 axb4+ ♘xb4+ 10 ♘xb4 ♔xb4 11 ♔d4 ♔b3 12 f4 ♔c2 13 ♔e5 ♔d3 14 ♔f6 ♔e3 15 ♔g7 ♔f3 16 ♔xh7 ♔g2 17 ♔xg6 ♔xh2 18 ♔xf5, and White wins. This process – the changing of one type of advantage for another – is called transforming an advantage.

Black declines the sacrificial offer, and the next stage commences: the struggle to advance the pawn.

8 ... axb4 9 axb4+ ♔d6 10 ♔d4 ♘c7 11 f4 ♘b5+ 12 ♔c4 ♘c7

Black cannot play 12 ... ♔c6 on account of 13 ♘d4+.

13 ♘e3

This is undoubtedly the simplest: White strengthens the position of his pieces. 13 b5 also wins, but it demands lengthy calculation, since Black has the chance to give up his knight for the pawn and create considerable complications. White would have to play very accurately to win; for example, 13 ... ♘xb5 14 ♔xb5 ♔d5 15 ♘e1 ♔e4 16 ♔c5 ♔e3 17 ♔d5 ♔f2 18

♔e5! (White gains valuable time by a knight counter-sacrifice) 18 ... ♔xe1 (if Black does not accept the sacrifice but continues 18 ... ♔g1, there follows 19 ♘f3+ ♔g2 20 ♔f6! ♔xf3 21 ♔g7, winning as in the main variation) 19 ♔f6 ♔f2 20 ♔g7 ♔g2 21 ♔xh7 ♔xh2 22 ♔xg6 ♔xg3 23 ♔xf5, and White wins.

Let us now return to the main line after **13 ♘e3**.

13 ... ♔c6 14 ♔d4 ♔d6 15 ♘c4+ ♔c6

If Black tries to stop the king from getting to the pawns on the right flank, then the b-pawn becomes dangerous. For example 15 ... ♔e6 16 ♘e5 ♔d6 17 ♘f7+ ♔e7 18 ♘g5 h6 19 ♘f3 ♔f6 (20 ♘h4 was threatened) 20 ♔c5 ♘e6+ 21 ♔d6 g5 22 b5 ♘d8 23 ♘d4 ♘b7+ 24 ♔c7 ♘c5 25 b6 ♔g6 26 ♔c6 ♘a6 27 b7, and White wins.

16 ♔e5 ♔b5 17 ♘e3 ♘a6

On 17 ... ♔xb4, simplest of all is 18 ♘d5+, transposing into a won pawn ending.

18 ♘d5 ♔c4 19 ♘f6 h5 20 ♘d5 ♘b8 21 ♘e7, and White eliminates all Black's kingside pawns.

Exploiting an extra pawn in knight endings proves an insoluble problem in three basic situations: when it is impossible to create a passed pawn; when the passed pawn cannot be supported; and when the king is unable to approach the opponent's pawns.

Given equal material, an outside passed pawn or the possibility of creating one is a most important positional advantage.

As we know already, a knight is not a long-range piece and it finds it hard to take part in play on both flanks at the same time: time is needed for it to get from one to the other. Therefore, if a knight tries to hold back an advanced passed pawn, it is practically chained to it.

We may confidently say that an outside passed pawn is no less important in knight endings than in pawn endings. Here is an example.

Chigorin-Marshall
119   Carlsbad 1907

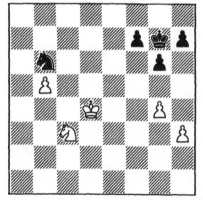

White has an outside passed pawn and can also prevent Black from creating a passed pawn on the other flank. The combination of these two factors allows White to achieve victory without difficulty.

1 ♘d5! ♘d7 2 g5! h6 3 ♘f6 ♘b6 4 h4 hxg5 5 hxg5 ♔f8 6 ♔c5 ♘a4+ 7 ♔d6!

The black king cannot get free.

7 ... ♔g7

If 7 ... ♘b6, then 8 ♘d7+ decides the issue.

8 ♔c6 ♔f8 9 b6 ♘xb6 10 ♔xb6 ♔e7 11 ♔c7 ♔f8

The attempt to attack White's pawn is not successful: 11 ... ♔e6 12 ♔d8 ♔f5 13 ♘h7 and wins.

12 ♔d7 ♔g7

The black king is trying to 'sit it out' in his fortress, but White overcomes the final barrier.

13 ♔e7 ♔h8 14 ♘e8

Of course, not 14 ♔xf7?? stalemate.

14 ... ♔g8 15 ♔f6 and Black resigned, for he loses his pawns.

By analogy with pawn endings, the strong position of the king is an important advantage in knight endings.

In Position 120 the white king is able to come into play quickly and attack the c-pawn. The opponent's king is more passively placed, and this determines White's

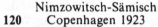

Nimzowitsch-Sämisch
120   Copenhagen 1923

decisive advantage.

1 ♔f3 ♔f7 2 ♘c3

2 ♔e4 ♔e6 3 g4 is simpler. Then White plays 4 ♘c3 and in the end he wins the c-pawn, and with it the game.

2 ... ♘d4+ 3 ♔e4 ♘b3 4 ♔d5

At first sight White has significantly strengthened his position. But in fact his king has moved away from the kingside pawns, which may allow the black knight to create counter-threats there.

4 ... ♘d2 5 h3

In this way White prevents the fixing of his pawns by ... g4.

5 ... f5 6 ♘d1 ♔f6 7 ♘e3 ♘e4 8 ♘xc4 ♘xf2 9 b4

White has transformed one type of advantage into another:

he has acquired an outside passed pawn. But Black too has his counterchances.

9 ... ♔e7

Only after this incorrect move is White able to realise his advantage without difficulty. It was essential to play actively with 9 ... ♘e4!, for example: 10 b5 ♘c3+ 11 ♔c6 ♘xb5! 12 ♔xb5 f4, with good drawing chances.

10 b5 ♔d7 11 b6 ♘e4

Too late. Now the knight no longer has time to pursue active operations on the other wing, but must hurry to the help of its king.

12 ♘e5+ ♔c8 13 ♔c6 ♘f6 14 ♘d3!

Threatening 15 b7+ ♔b8 16 ♘c5.

14 ... ♘d7 15 b7+ ♔d8 16 ♔d6 ♘b8 17 ♘b4 ♘d7 18 ♘c6+ ♔e8 19 ♔c7, and **Black resigned**.

Bishop Endings

Bishops of the Same Colour

In endings with bishops of the same colour, just as in knight endings, an extra pawn proves a decisive advantage, provided that other things are equal.

The winning plan here is approximately the same as in knight endings: one must create a passed pawn and queen it. A thorough examination of the following example will acquaint us with the characteristics of these endings.

121

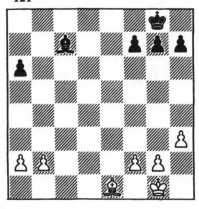

1 ♔f1 ♚f8 2 ♔e2 ♚e7 3 ♔d3 ♚d6 4 ♔c4 ♚c6 5 ♗c3 g6 6 b4 ♗b6 7 f3 ♗c7 8 a4 ♗b6 9 ♗d4

The mobilisation of forces prior to creating a passed pawn has been completed. Both White's bishop and king occupy fine positions.

9 ... ♗c7 10 b5+ axb5+ 11 axb5+ ♚b7

The attempt to prevent the advance of the white king loses at once: 11 ... ♚d6 is followed by 12 ♗c5+ ♚d7 13 b6 ♗g3 14 ♚d5 ♗f4 15 ♗d4 and 16 ♗e5.

12 ♚d5

It is all going according to plan.

The black king has been diverted by the passed pawn, and White is ready to attack the enemy pawns on the kingside. However, as distinct from both knight and pawn endings, here the play is not yet over. White still has another hurdle to overcome. The bishop is a long-range piece, and by controlling the approaches to his pawns, Black tries not to allow the hostile invasion. In order to win White must free the way for his king.

12 ... ♗b8

After 12 ... ♗f4 13 ♗e5 ♗e3 14 ♚d6 White immediately carries out the invasion. But now 13 ♗e5 ♗a7 14 ♚d6 achieves nothing, as it is answered by 14 ... ♗b8+, and the white king has to go back again. Nor could it force its way through after 14 ♗d6 ♗f2! 15 ♚e5 ♗g3+. How then is White to drive off his opponent's bishop?

It is once again useful to compare this ending with the knight and the pawn endings. In those, as soon as the weaker side's king was driven back, the limited mobility of his pieces told against him. The weaker side got into zugzwang and was compelled through lack of moves to allow the opponent's king to reach his pawns. In this case there is no zugzwang as yet, and the bishop can manoeuvre quietly, guarding the approaches to its camp.

But is it not possible here, too, to limit the mobility of the bishop even further? It turns out that it is.

13 ♗f2! ♗c7 14 g3 h5 15 h4

But not 15 f4? h4.

15 ... ♗b8 16 b6!

The task has been fulfilled. Black has been reduced to zugzwang and cannot defend himself against the manoeuvre 17 f4 followed by 18 ♗d4 and 19 ♗e5 with its transposition into a won pawn ending. 16 ... ♔c8 does not help on account of 17 ♔c6 ♗e5 18 f4 ♗b8 19 b7+ ♔d8 20 ♗b6+ and 21 ♗c7, with an easy win.

We have established that compared with knight and, in particular, pawn endings there are additional difficulties in bishop endings which complicate the task of exploiting an extra pawn. Even in this ideal example White needed to show great inventiveness in order to bring about a zugzwang position and penetrate with his king into the enemy camp.

If it is impossible to obtain a zugzwang position and the bishop succeeds in defending the approaches to the pawns on the other wing, such an ending may end in a draw.

As far as the assessment of a position with equal material is concerned, one of the main guides

is the presence of an outside passed pawn. Here is an example on this theme.

122　　Lisitsyn-Levenfish
　　　Leningrad 1932　　　**B**

In addition to the outside passed pawn which Black has in this position, White's h-pawn is fixed on a square of the same colour as his bishop and must be defended. Black's chances are reduced by the fact there is comparatively little material left on the board and the promoting square of his h-pawn is inaccessible to his bishop.

1 ... ♗f6!

After this White immediately gets into zugzwang. Bishop moves lead either to the loss of a pawn or the advance of Black's passed pawn, while 2 ♔e2 is followed by 2 ... ♔f4.

2 f4 ♗b2

Only a draw results from 2 ...
♔g4 3 ♔e4 ♗e7 4 f5 b4 (or 4 ...
♗f6 5 ♔d5 ♔xf5 6 ♔c6 ♔g4 7
♔xb5 ♗xh4 8 ♗a5 ♗g3 9 ♗d8
♗f4 10 ♔c4 ♗g5 11 ♗xg5 and 12
♔d3) 5 f6! ♗f8 6 f7 b3 7 ♔d3.

**3 ♗d2 ♗g7 4 ♗b4 ♗f6 5 ♗e1
♗e7!**

Again it is zugzwang. The king
has to move.

6 ♔f3 ♗d6 7 ♗d2 ♗c7!

Tied to the defence of the
pawn, White is once more forced
to make poor moves. Against
bishop moves on the c1-e3 diagonal
... b4 is decisive, while if 8 ♔g3,
then 8 ... ♔e4 wins. he therefore
prefers to part with the f-pawn.

**8 ♗c3 ♗xf4 9 ♗b4 ♗e5 10 ♗a5
♗f6 11 ♗e1 ♗e7!**

By repeatedly exploiting zugzwang Black gradually increases
his advantage. This time White
must fall back.

12 ♔g3 ♔e4

Moving the king over to the b-
pawn is decisive. For example:

**13 ♗a5 ♔d3 14 ♗e1 ♔c4 15
♔f4 ♗f6 16 ♔f5 ♗c3 17 ♗g3 b4
18 ♗d6 b3 19 ♗a3 ♔d3 20 ♔g5
♔c2 21 ♔xh5 ♗d2 22 ♔g4 ♗c1**,
and Black wins.

We have established that in the
above example the location of

pawns on squares of the same
colour as the bishop was a
substantial deficiency in the position. This is true, as a rule, of the
majority of bishop endings. In the
first place, such pawns require
protection, which fetters the powers of the defending side; in the
second, the squares between the
pawns cannot be touched by the
bishop, and that may permit the
opponent's king to approach the
pawns.

In positions of this type the win
– if it is possible at all – is usually
achieved by setting up zugzwang.
Here is a characteristic example.

123

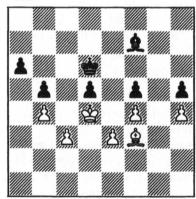

Black's defensive resources are
nearly at an end. The bishop
protects the weak pawns, while
the king guards the entry squares.
White's task is to transfer the turn
to move to his opponent. For
then Black would either have to

give up a pawn or let the king through, and in either case this would lead to a quick defeat.

In order to establish the defensive possibilities, let us try manoeuvring with the bishop:

1 ♗e2 ♗e8!

It transpires that Black has only one correct reply which will prolong the resistance. After 1 ... ♗g6 2 ♗d3 ♗h7 3 ♗f1! he immediately ends up in zugzwang: 3 ... ♗g6 is met by 4 ♗g2 ♗f7 5 ♗f3 and 3 ... ♗g8 by 4 ♗e2 ♗f7 5 ♗f3.

2 ♗d3 ♗g6

Again the best move. On 2 ... ♗d7 there follows 3 ♗c2 ♗e6 (3 ... ♗c8 4 ♗d1, winning a pawn) 4 ♗d1 ♗f7 5 ♗f3.

3 ♗c2 ♗h7

The reader will no doubt have noticed that each time Black has to make a single, forced move. It is not hard to guess that we have here another case of corresponding squares – to each move of the white bishop there corresponds only one move by Black's bishop. We can say that f7 corresponds to f3, e8 to e2, g6 to d3, and h7 to c2. But White has a decisive manoeuvre, which breaks the correspondence and places Black in a position of zugzwang.

4 ♗b3! ♗g8 5 ♗d1! ♗f7, and

White wins.

Bishops of Opposite Colours

In endings with bishops of opposite colours a material advantage often does not have a decisive significance. An extra pawn, sometimes even two or three, may prove insufficient to win the game.

Let us consider, for example, a typical position in which White has an extra pawn. White won the analogous position with bishops of the same colour. But here we have an elementary draw.

124

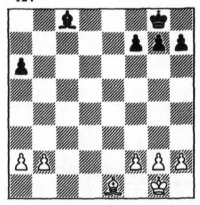

Let us verify this: **1 ♔f1 ♔f8 2 ♔e2 ♔e7 3 ♔d3 ♗e6 4 b3**

If 4 a4, there follows 4 ... ♗b3 5 a5 ♗a4, and the extra pawn plays no part at all.

4 ... ♔d6 5 ♗b4+ ♔c6 6 ♔c3 g6

7 a4 ♔b6 8 ♗f8 h5 9 b4 ♗d5 10 g3 ♗e6

Certain conclusions can now be drawn. White cannot even create a passed pawn. But perhaps it is possible to force a way through with the king to the pawns on the other wing?

11 ♔d4 ♗b3!

It is useful to immobilise the pawns.

12 a5+ ♔b5 13 ♔e5 ♗e6 14 ♔f6 ♔c6

At this point we can draw another important conclusion. Black's king has been diverted, but the bishop alone copes excellently with the defence of the pawns.

15 ♔g5 ♔b5 16 h4 ♔c6 17 f3 ♗d5!

Though it is a drawn ending, Black still has to play carefully. 18 g4! was threatened, creating a dangerous passed pawn on the h-file that would guarantee victory.

18 ♔f4 ♔b5 19 g4 ♔c6 20 gxh5 gxh5

And there is nothing more that White can undertake.

This example provides a graphic demonstration of the peculiarities of endings with bishops of opposite colours. The first special characteristic consists in the fact that the advance of a passed pawn cannot be supported by the bishop, as the squares attacked by the enemy bishop are inaccessible to it. The second is that the bishop cannot attack enemy pawns situated on squares of the opposite colour. Therefore, if the weaker side's king can occupy a square in front of the pawn that is inaccessible to the opponent's bishop and at the same time defend his pawns on both flanks with the bishop, then the game cannot be won. These special features determine the three basic drawn positions characteristic of this ending. The following position is typical:

125

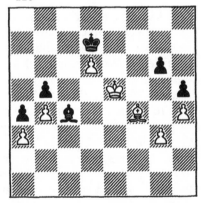

To draw, it is sufficient for Black to 'mark time' on the spot. White is powerless to undertake anything. His king may wander over the whole board, but it will not bring him any success: Black's bishop on its own, without the help of the king, copes excellently with the defence of the pawns on both wings. And here is another drawn position:

126

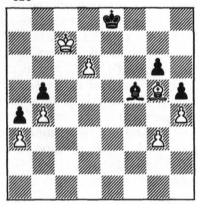

In this case Black's pieces are less favourably placed than in the position on the previous diagram. Nevertheless, White cannot achieve anything. Only the minimum of accuracy is demanded of Black: thus, in reply to **1 ♔b6**, he must not play 1 ... ♗d3?? 2 ♔c6!, when White wins, but **1 ... ♗d7**. It is characteristic of both the positions considered above that the bishop alone can defend the weaknesses on the flanks.

The advance of passed pawns in endings with bishops of opposite colours can only be supported by the king. Therefore, if the defending side is able to prevent the king from getting to these pawns, then,

as a rule, it proves impossible to win.

127

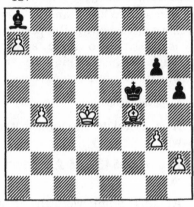

Diagram 127 shows another typical drawn position. White cannot exploit his great material superiority, since his king's invasion is blocked by the black king. For example:

1 ♔c5 ♔e6! 2 ♔b6 ♔d7! 3 b5 ♔c8!

3 ... ♗f3 would have been a bad mistake on account of 4 a8=♕! ♗xa8 5 ♔a7 ♗f3 6 ♔b8! (White has returned part of his material advantage, but has forced a way through with his king and can support the advance of the b-pawn) 6 ... ♗g2 7 b6 ♔c6 8 ♔a7 and wins.

In the positions that we have looked at so far the defending side has kept in the main to passive tactics. But in this last position only an active defence saves the game. The weaker side's king must manoeuvre "on guard at its frontiers" and not allow the enemy king to advance.

A legitimate question may occur to the reader: "In what instance can an ending with bishops of opposite colours be won?"

The following example answers this question.

Kotov–Botvinnik
128 Moscow 1955

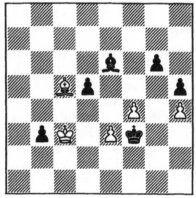

Apparently, we have before us a typical drawn position: the king contends with Black's passed pawn, while the bishop defends the pawns on both sides.

However, Black can create another passed pawn, and that is decisive.

1 ... g5!! 2 fxg5

White also loses after 2 hxg5 h4 3 ♗d6 ♗f5 4 g6 ♗xg6 5 f5 ♗xf5 6 ♔xb3 ♔g2, when he must give up his bishop for the h-pawn.

2 ... d4+!

It is important for Black to preserve his b-pawn.

3 exd4 ♔g3 4 ♗a3

4 ♗e7 ♔xh4 5 g6+ ♔g4 does not help either.

4 ... ♔xh4 5 ♔d3 ♔xg5 6 ♔e4 h4 7 ♔f3 ♗d5+ and White resigned.

This example shows vividly that it is not a material advantage which is important in endings with bishops of opposite colours but rather how effectively the kings can support their passed pawns.

Endings with Bishop versus Knight

The possibilities open to bishop and knight were shown earlier during our examination of the respective knight and bishop endings. Now we shall mainly consider the special features of the struggle of these pieces against each other.

An extra pawn, whether on the side of the bishop or the knight, is a great and, as a rule, decisive advantage. Exploiting the material advantage is accomplished according to the well-known plan: one should create a passed pawn and queen it. We shall acquaint ourselves with the individual elements of this plan in the course of analysing examples.

Bonch Osmolovsky-Konstantinopolsky
129   Moscow 1949

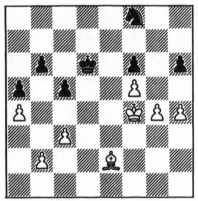

In diagram 129 all is ready for White to create a passed pawn, and there followed:

1 g5 hxg5+ 2 hxg5 fxg5+ 3 ♔xg5 ♔e5 4 ♗d3

White avoids the trap: 4 f6? loses a pawn after 4 ... ♘h7+.

4 ... ♘d7 5 ♔g6 ♘f6 6 ♔f7

The further advance of the pawn is impossible, for the f6 square is inaccessible to the bishop. Therefore, by exploiting the fact that Black's pieces have been diverted by the struggle with the pawn, White sets off with his king on a long, roundabout route towards the opponent's pawns.

6 ... ♘d5 7 ♗c4 ♘e3 8 ♗e6 ♘g4

8 ... ♘xf5 results in a hopeless pawn ending.

9 ♔e7 ♘f6 10 ♗c8 ♘e4 11 ♔d7 ♔xf5 12 ♔c6+ ♔e5 13 ♔xb6

Having forced its way through to the pawns, the white king begins to eliminate them.

13 ... ♘d6 14 ♗a6 ♔d5 15 ♗b5

White is in no hurry, for the black pawns are doomed.

15 ... ♘c8+ 16 ♔xa5 ♔d6 17 ♗a6 ♘e7 18 ♔b6 ♘d5+ 19 ♔b7 ♘e3 20 ♗e2 c4 21 a5 and Black resigned.

If the material superiority is on the side of the knight, the method of exploiting it is in its most general features the same. Here, however, one is both ill advised to be in a particular hurry to create a passed pawn and, still more so, to advance it. This may not lead to a lessening of the mobility of the bishop, it being a long-range piece. First, it is important to achieve a weakening of the opponent's pawn formation, in order either to divert the opposing forces from the passed pawn or to create breakthrough points for the passage of the king to the enemy pawns. Here is a typical example (diagram 130).

It is difficult for White to effect an immediate advance of the passed pawn. 1 ♘b5 ♗f2 2 d5+ ♔d7, for instance, would be a

Levenfish-Rauzer
130 Tbilisi 1937

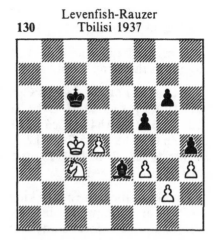

mistake, as White cannot easily strengthen his position after that. The correct procedure is to attack the enemy pawns first.

1 ♘d5! ♗g5 2 f4! ♗d8 3 ♘b4+ ♚d6 4 ♘d3 g5

After 4 ... ♚e6 5 ♘e5 ♚f6 6 ♚c5 the way is opened up for the d-pawn.

5 ♘e5 ♚e6 6 d5+ ♚f6 7 ♚c5 gxf4 8 ♘c6 and **Black resigned**, since he cannot stop the pawn without suffering decisive material losses.

When it comes to assessing situations with level material, an important role is played by positional factors already well known to us: an outside passed pawn; weaknesses in the pawn formation. Accordingly, we shall examine only those points which are specially characteristic of the given distribution of forces.

The bishop is particularly good at combating the knight in an open position, where the pawns are not blocked and it has freedom to manoeuvre. It stands to reason that here, too, the position of the king has an important significance. An active king working in harmony with a bishop represents a mighty force. The analysis of the following example should convince one of this.

Stoltz-Kashdan
131 The Hague 1928 **B**

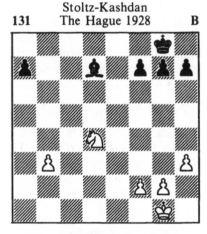

Although Black's advantage here is great, it is not easy to discern. There would not appear to be any weakness in White's game, and his knight is beautifully placed. However, a quick glance does not give a correct appraisal of the position. Let us examine how the play went.

1 ... ♚f8 2 ♚f1 ♚e7 3 ♚e2 ♚d6 4 ♚d3 ♚d5

This is the first important point. Thanks to the fact that it was his turn to move, Black has occupied a more active position with his king.

5 h4 ♗c8!

Black transfers his bishop to a6, a square from which it restrains White's pieces and prepares to threaten his g-pawn.

6 ♘f3 ♗a6+ 7 ♔c3

If 7 ♔e3, the black king pushes through to the b-pawn: after 7 ... ♔c5 8 ♘g5 ♔b4 9 ♘xf7 ♔xb3 Black obtains a dangerous outside passed pawn, which is a decisive advantage in such a position.

7 ... h6 8 ♘d4 g6 9 ♘c2 ♔e4

Black's advantage is beginning to stand out more and more. His king has improved its position still further, having taken up a preparatory post for an attack on the enemy pawns.

10 ♘e3 f5 11 ♔d2 f4

By advancing his f-pawn Black has dislodged the white knight. Now 12 ♘c2 is followed by 12 ... ♗f1! 13 ♘e1 ♔f5 14 f3 g5 15 hxg5 ♔xg5, and the black king penetrates to g3.
Realising that passive defence will do him no good, White tries unsuccessfully to go over to the counterattack.

12 ♘g4 h5 13 ♘f6+ ♔f5 14 ♘d7 ♗c8! 15 ♘f8 g5! 16 g3

After 16 hxg5 the knight is caught in the "trap" and lost.

16 ... gxh4 17 gxh4 ♔g4 18 ♘g6 ♗f5 19 ♘e7 ♗e6 20 b4 ♔xh4 21 ♔d3 ♔g4 22 ♔e4 h4 23 ♘c6 ♗f5+ 24 ♔d5 f3 25 b5 h3 26 ♘xa7 h2 27 b6 h1=♕ 28 ♘c6 ♕b1 29 ♔c5 ♗e4 White resigned

Thanks to the more active king position and a powerful bishop, Black was able to force a way into his opponent's camp with his king, and this made it a foregone conclusion that he would win. The assessment of the position was based on Black's active, i.e. dynamic, possibilities. He was able to strengthen his position, until it led to a decisive material advantage. The plan that Black employed is typical of these positions. It consists of the following basic stages:

a) The king gets as near as possible to the opponent's pawn lines.

b) Entry squares are created in his camp.

c) The bishop strives to limit the activity of the opponent's pieces; forced to defend the approaches to their camp, these pieces become less active and are gradually thrust back.

d) The king breaks into the

opponent's position and secures a decisive material advantage.

There are positions in which it is the knight that plays an equally dominant role. The following is an example:

Averbakh-Lilienthal
132   Moscow 1949

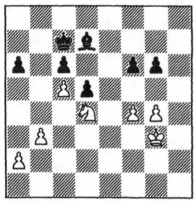

Although Black has a protected passed pawn here, it has no bearing on the assessment of the position because the knight, while keeping it securely blockaded, at the same time takes a most active part in the play. Black's bishop is considerably less active on account of the necessity to protect his pawns, and the same can be said of Black's king.

White is able to open a way into the enemy camp by **1 g5!** and win the game. Play continued as follows:

1 ... fxg5

Black could have prevented the advance of the white king for the moment by playing 1 ... f5. In that case the win is reached by 2 ♘f3 ♗e8 3 ♘e5 ♔d8 4 ♔f3 ♔e7 5 ♔e3 ♔e6 6 ♔d4 ♔e7 7 ♘d3! ♔e6 8 ♘b4 a5 9 ♘d3 ♗d7 10 a4 ♗e8 11 b4 axb4 12 ♘xb4.

2 fxg5 ♗c8 3 ♔f4

At this point the game was adjourned, and **Black resigned** without resuming – on account of the following variation: 3 ... a5 4 ♔e5 ♗g4 (4 ... ♗a6 could be answered by 5 ♔f6 ♗d3 6 ♔e7 and then 7 ♘e6+, still further confining the black king) 5 ♔f6 ♗h5 6 ♔e7 ♗g4 7 a3! ♗d1 8 ♘e6+ ♔b7 9 ♔d6 ♗xb3 10 ♘d8+ ♔c8 11 ♘xc6 a4 12 ♘e7+, and White wins.

Rook Endings

The degree of activity of the rook – being the powerful piece it is – is an essential factor in the assessment of the position. As a rule, material advantage can only be exploited successfully if one's rook is actively placed. A worsening of its position may have a substantial effect on the situation, neutralising the significance of a material advantage. Consider the following example.

Alekhine-Capablanca
133   Buenos Aires 1927

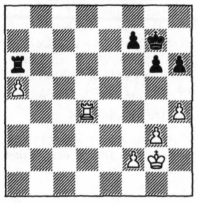

White is an outside passed pawn to the good. It is blocked by the opponent's rook and since it is also attacked, it must be defended. There followed:

1 ♖a4!

A very strong move! The rook is especially strong here, stationed behind the passed pawn and, as it were, 'pushing' it from behind. Owing to this the black rook is forced to remain passive, for otherwise the pawn will move forward.

Now White threatens to bring his king over to the pawn and drive away the rook. So the black king must come to the relief of the rook.

1 ... ♔f6 2 ♔f3 ♔e5 3 ♔e3 h5 4 ♔d3 ♔d5 5 ♔c3 ♔c5

So far Black has managed to

prevent his opponent's king from reaching the pawn.

6 ♖a2!

White's plan becomes clear. He waits until Black's useful moves are exhausted and he gets into zugzwang. Black cannot win the a-pawn, as that leads to a hopeless pawn ending. While if 6 ... ♖a8, then 7 a6 strengthens White's position even more. In an attempt to find some chances, Capablanca decides to regroup, leaving his king to act as the pawn's blockader and freeing his rook for active operations.

6 ... ♔b5 7 ♔d4!

Exploiting the fact that the black king has been diverted to contend with the passed pawn, White advances towards the pawns on the other flank. We have already met this idea more than once during our analysis of minor piece endings.

7 ... ♖d6+ 8 ♔e5 ♖e6+ 9 ♔f4 ♔a6 10 ♔g5!

White has achieved a great success: his king has forced its way into the opposing pawn position. Because of this, it seems to me that Black's 3rd move was faulty, for he needlessly weakened the approaches to his pawns and so eased White's task.

10 ... ♖e5+ 11 ♔h6 ♖f5 12 f4

As Alekhine himself pointed out, playing for zugzwang wins more quickly: 12 ♔g7 ♖f3 13 ♔g8! ♖f6 14 ♔f8 ♖f3 15 ♔g7 ♖f5 16 f4!, and Black has no useful moves. After the text move Black is able to prolong his resistance a little.

12 ... ♖c5! 13 ♖a3 ♖c7 14 ♔g7 ♖d7 15 f5! gxf5 16 ♔h6 f4!

Black defends himself desperately!

17 gxf4 ♖d5 18 ♔g7 ♖f5 19 ♖a4 ♔b5 20 ♖e4!

This is the decisive move. The a-pawn has played its diversionary role and can now be given up with a clear conscience.

20 ... ♔a6 21 ♔h6 ♖xa5

White also wins after 21 ... ♔b7 22 ♖e5 ♖xf4 23 ♔xh5.

22 ♖e5 ♖a1 23 ♔xh5 ♖g1 24 ♖g5 ♖h1 25 ♖f5 ♔b6

The distant position of his king ruins Black. Were it, say, on g7, he would have excellent chances of a draw.

26 ♖xf7 ♔c6 27 ♖e7! Black resigned

His king is cut off and cannot take part in the struggle against the pawns.

We have thus established that the method of exploiting an extra pawn which we examined in minor piece endings is also applicable here. The stronger side creates a passed pawn and attempts to advance it. If the rook opposes it, then he moves his king over to the pawn and with the help of his rook escorts the pawn forward. If the king opposes it, then in order to win it is necessary to penetrate the opponent's lines on the other wing so as to make use of the diversion of his forces and gain a decisive material advantage. This is exactly what occurred in the preceding game.

Even with the stronger side's rook favourably placed, considerable resistance has to be overcome in order to exploit a material advantage. When the rook is less actively placed, the task becomes many times more complicated. Take the following example.

134

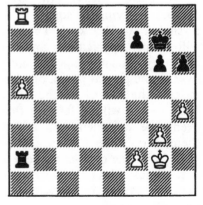

Here the position of the rooks has been changed compared with the previous example. The weaker side's rook attacks the passed pawn from the rear, whilst the stronger side's defends his pawn from the front. Such an arrangement of pieces favours the defending side, since his rook can fulfil two tasks at the same time: contend with the passed pawn and attack the opponent's pawns on the other wing.

How is White to exploit his extra pawn? He can advance the pawn to a7, but that will not improve his chances, since his rook will be unable to get away from a8. Nor will moving the king up to the pawn at a7 help in that case, for as soon as it reaches b6 or b7 the rook will drive it away from the pawn by checking from the rear and then take up its post behind the pawn again.

White can try leaving the pawn on a6, preserving the square a7 as a 'shelter' for his king. Then he will come up against another difficulty. In moving the king over to the passed pawn, one has to cast the pawns on the other wing to the will of fate. In that event the opponent can attack them and, while the king is *en route*, win one or two of them.

If Black plays actively, this plan too cannot be realised. For example:

1 a6 ♔f6 2 ♔f3 h5 3 ♔e3

After 3 ♔e4 ♖xf2 4 ♔d5 ♖a2! 5 ♔c6 ♔f5 6 ♔b7 ♔g4 7 ♖f8 ♔xg3 8 a7 ♔xh4 9 ♖xf7 g5 10 a8=♕ ♖xa8 11 ♔xa8 White has won the rook, but only at the risk of losing the game.

3 ... ♔f5 4 f3 ♖a3+ 5 ♔d4 ♖xf3 6 ♖f8

This is better than 6 ♔c5 ♖a3 7 ♔b6 ♔g4.

6 ... ♖a3 7 ♖xf7+ ♔g4 8 ♖f6 ♔xg3 9 ♖xg6+ ♔xh4

Black has attained material equality, but the rather poor position of his king complicates the defence.

10 ♔c5 ♔h3 11 ♔b6 h4

Black must hurry, for in positions where there are passed pawns every tempo is usually valuable.

12 ♖g5 ♖xa6+

This is the simplest. However, 12 ... ♔h2 does not lose either, e.g. 13 ♖a5 ♖xa5 14 ♔xa5 h3 15 a7 ♔g1 16 a8=♕ h2, and as we know, Black secures a draw.

13 ♔xa6 ♔h2 14 ♔b5 h3 15 ♔c4 ♔h1 16 ♔d3 h2 17 ♔e2 stalemate

Different possibilities may arise depending on the pawn configuration, but in every case it is active counterplay against the pawns on the other wing that provides the key to safety.

Victory can be achieved in these endings, where the weaker side's rook attacks the pawn from the rear, if the weaker side is late in organising counterplay or it is possible to attack pawn weaknesses on the other wing.

135

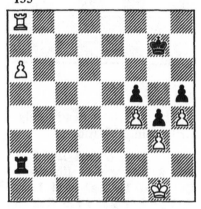

In the diagrammed position it would be dangerous for White to set off towards the a-pawn with his king, since Black, once he had won the g-pawn, would also have a passed pawn.

But **1 a7!** does lead to a win. Now Black's rook will no longer be able to eliminate the g-pawn, while the white king can head for the enemy f-pawn. Here is a possible variation:

1 ... ♔h7 2 ♔f1 ♔g7 3 ♔e1 ♔h7 4 ♔d1 ♔g7 5 ♔c1 ♔h7 6 ♔b1 ♖a5 7 ♔b2 ♔g7 8 ♔b3 ♔h7 9 ♔b4 ♖a1

10 ♔c5 ♔g7 11 ♔d5

11 ♔b6 is senseless on account of 11 ... ♖b1+.

11 ... ♖a2 12 ♔e5 ♖a5+ 13 ♔e6

Black is in zugzwang and loses a pawn.

13 ... ♖a6+ 14 ♔xf5 ♖a5+ 15 ♔e6 ♖a6+ 16 ♔e7 ♖a1 17 f5 ♖e1+ 18 ♔d6 ♖a1 19 f6+ ♔f7 20 ♖h8 ♖xa7 21 ♖h7+, and White wins.

There is one more important position that needs to be examined. This is where the rook defends the passed pawn not from the front but from the side. In that case the result is determined by whether or not the rook can take part in the defence of one's pawns and so free the king to move up to the passed pawn. Here is an appropriate example.

Averbakh-Euwe
136   Zürich 1953

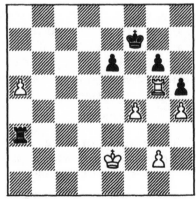

Black's position is hopeless, since he cannot prevent the white king from moving over to the passed pawn. White's actively placed rook not only defends all his pawns but also, by attacking the g-pawn, restrains the black king. Play continued: **1 ♔d2 ♔e7 2 ♔c2!**. White's a-pawn is too strong for it to be exchanged for the g-pawn.

2 ... ♔d6 3 ♔b2 ♖a4 4 g3 ♔c6 5 ♔b3 ♖a1 6 ♔b4 ♖b1+ 7 ♔c4 ♖a1 8 ♔b3 Black resigned

He either loses another pawn or must allow the white king to reach the a-pawn, which is also equivalent to defeat.

Such a multitude of pawn configurations are encountered in practice that in a short space it is impossible to examine even those pawn structures which are met most often. We shall now consider a case with all the pawns on one wing.

The chances of winning from diagram 137 are insignificant and may only be realised if Black defends weakly. Keres played correctly and easily obtained a draw. This is how it went:

1 ... h5!

The advance of the g- and h-pawns comes into White's plan, so Black stops it beforehand.

2 ♖c2 ♔g7 3 ♔g2 ♖b5 4 ♔f3

137 Petrosian-Keres
Moscow 1951   **B**

♔f6 5 h4

5 h3 and 6 g4 leads only to further simplification.

5 ... ♖f5+ 6 ♔g2 ♖a5 7 ♔h3 ♖a4 8 ♖d2 ♔e5 9 ♖b2 ♔f6 10 ♖b5 ♖a2 11 ♔g2 ♖a4 12 ♔f3 ♖a3 13 ♔f4 ♖a2 14 f3 ♖e2 15 e4

After lengthy manoeuvres White has at last begun to push up his pawns.

15 ... ♖e1 16 ♖b6+ ♔g7 17 ♖a6 ♖b1 18 ♖c6 ♖g1 19 ♖c2 ♔f6 20 ♖a2 ♔g7 21 ♖e2 ♔f6 22 ♖e3 ♔g7 23 e5 ♔f8 24 g4 hxg4 25 fxg4 ♔g7 26 ♔g5 ♖f1 27 ♖e4 ♖f3 28 h5 gxh5 29 gxh5

A passed pawn has materialised, but it does not bring with it any decisive improvement to White's chances.

29 ... f6+ 30 ♔g4 ♖f1 31 h6+

A last trap. If 31 ... ♔xh6, then 32 e6! f4+ 33 ♔h3! fxe4 34 e7.

31 ... ♔g6!, and a **draw** was agreed.

We have already observed several times how the active position of the rook compensates for material losses. Here is another example on this theme.

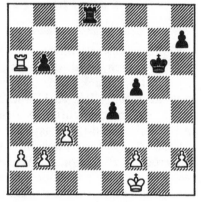

Tarrasch-Rubinstein
138 San Sebastián 1911 **B**

Here passive defence by 1 ... ♖d6 loses quickly because of 2 ♔e2 followed by 3 a4, threatening 4 a5. Black's salvation is in active play.

1 ... ♖d2! 2 ♖xb6+ ♔g5

White has two extra pawns, but Black threatens to construct a mating net around the white king by ... f4-f3. For example, 3 a4 f4 4 a5 f3 5 ♔e1 ♖e2+, and Black forces a repetition of moves, since 6 ♔d1 ♖xf2 7 a6 e3 8 a7 ♖d2+ 9

♔c1 f2, etc. is dangerous for White. The latter, therefore, must think of defence.

3 ♔e1 ♖c2 4 ♖b5! ♔g4! 5 h3+!

To permit 5 ... f4 and 6 ... ♔f3 could only lead to a loss for White.

5 ... ♔xh3 6 ♖xf5 ♖xb2 7 ♖f4 ♖xa2 8 ♖xe4 h5

White has neutralised Black's main threat, but Black has one more trump left – the passed h-pawn.

9 c4 ♔g2 10 ♖f4 ♖c2 11 ♖h4 ♔f3 12 ♔d1 ♖xf2 13 c5 ♔e3 14 ♖xh5 ♔d4 Drawn

Now we shall examine a number of positions where material is equal but one side has a positional advantage.

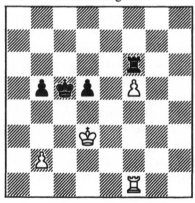

Lasker-Rubinstein
139 St Petersburg 1914

Two factors determine White's

positional advantage. He has an outside passed pawn and Black's rook is in a passive position. We have more than once convinced ourselves of the disadvantage of blockading a passed pawn with a rook: it loses greatly in strength. The presence of an outside passed pawn is not in itself a decisive advantage in a rook ending. We have only to interchange the positions of the rooks to be satisfied of this at once, but in conjunction with the passive placing of the opponent's rook an outside passed pawn has a substantial effect on the assessment of the position. In this case Black is unable to save the game.

Play continued: **1 ♖f4 b4**.

Black is in zugzwang.

2 b3 ♖f7 3 f6 ♔d6 4 ♔d4 ♔e6 5 ♖f2 ♔d6 6 ♖a2! ♖c7 7 ♖a6+ ♔d7 8 ♖b6, and **Black resigned**.

The presence of weak pawns represents a serious positional defect in rook endings, as it does in others, for the pieces that are forced to defend the weak pawns lose much of their strength. Weaknesses, therefore, are not only bad in themselves but also because they have an adverse effect upon the activity of the king and particularly the rook. Below is an interesting example on this theme.

140　　Marshall-Chigorin
　　　　　Barmen 1905　　　　**B**

White has weak pawns at a3 and d4 which need defending. Apparently, Black can win a pawn at once by 1 ... ♖c3+ and 2 ... ♖xa3. However, after 2 ♔e4 and 3 ♔d5 the d-pawn is transformed from a weak pawn into a dangerous passed pawn, and White has every right to count on a happy outcome to the game. Black correctly declined the sacrifice and played **1 ... ♔e6!**, reckoning that the pawn would not run away and that it was necessary to improve the position of his king. In rook endings the activity of pieces is generally worth more than an extra pawn.

2 ♖b3 ♔d5 3 ♖d3 f5 4 h3 h5 5 ♔e2

White is in zugzwang; he would also have had to give up a pawn after 5 h4 g6.

5 ... ⃞xd4 6 ⃞c3 ⃞e4+ 7 ⃞d2 h4 8 ⃞c7

He makes a desperate attempt to go over to the counter-attack.

8 ... hxg3 9 ⃞xg7 ⃞xf4 10 ⃞xg3 ⃞e5 11 ⃞e2 ⃞c4 12 ⃞g6 ⃞a4 13 ⃞g3 f4 14 ⃞b3 ⃞c4

14 ... ⃞e4? would be a bad mistake, as after 15 ⃞b4+ the pawn ending must end in a draw.

15 ⃞d1 ⃞e4 16 h4 f3 17 ⃞e1 ⃞f4 18 h5 ⃞c1+ 19 ⃞f2 ⃞c2+ 20 ⃞e1 ⃞g3, and **Black won.**

As we have already emphasized, the activity of the rook is one of the most important factors that determine the assessment of a rook ending. The roles played by material and positional advantages in the examples we have examined changed considerably according to the degree of activity of the rook. In the following position it is the very difference in the activity of the rooks that is decisive in reaching an assessment.

There are no doubts about White's positional advantage here. Black's rook is forced to defend the pawn at d6 and occupy a passive position. At the same time, his king must guard the g6 point against the entry of the white king. However, it is not zugzwang, as Black is able to move his rook up and down on the squares d8 and d7.

141 Forgacs-Bernstein
Coburg 1904

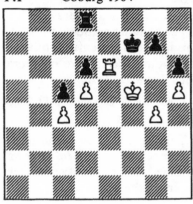

How is White to win? If his rook were on a6, then any move with it along the sixth rank, even with Black's rook on d7, would lead to zugzwang. Therefore, he played 1 ⃞e1, intending to transfer the rook to a6.

Now passive defence loses, so Black rightly decided to get his rook into action.

1 ... ⃞f8

He plans to answer 2 ⃞a1 with 2 ... ⃞e7+ 3 ⃞g6 ⃞f4!. For example 4 ⃞a7+ ⃞f8 5 ⃞a8+ ⃞e7 6 ⃞xg7 ⃞xg4+ 7 ⃞xh6 ⃞f6, and the excellent position of the black pieces prevents White from winning. If 2 ⃞e6, Black can continue 2 ... ⃞g8+ 3 ⃞g6 ⃞f4 4 ⃞e8+ ⃞f8, when the pawn ending is drawn.

White replied with **2 g5** and after **2 ... ⃞g8+ 3 ⃞g4 hxg5 4**

♔xg5 ♖f2! 5 ♖e6 ♖c2 6 ♖xd6 ♖xc4 the players soon acknowledged that it was a **draw**.

The winning manoeuvre, which Smyslov and Levenfish aptly call "extending the theatre of operations", is as follows:

1 g5! hxg5 2 ♔xg5 ♖d7 3 h6! gxh6+ 4 ♖xh6

This is the idea behind the exchange of pawns. The rook has obtained the possibility of attacking from the flank.

4 ... ♔g7 5 ♖g6+ ♔f7 6 ♔f5 ♖a7!

Black's only chance lies in a counter-attack.

7 ♖h6 ♔g7

Or 7 ... ♖a4 8 ♖h7+ ♔g8 9 ♖c7 ♖xc4 10 ♔e6 ♖e4+ 11 ♔xd6 c4 12 ♔c6 c3 13 d6! c2 14 ♔d7 ♖e2 15 ♔d8, and White wins.

8 ♖xd6 ♖a4 9 ♖d7+ ♔f8 10 ♔e6 ♖xc4 11 ♖d8+ ♔g7 12 d6

And as the reader may satisfy himself, White queens the pawn.

A difference in the placing of the kings can also prove an important factor and have a substantial influence on the assessment of the position.

At first glance it is not easy to assess the players' chances in diagram 142. White must lose a pawn, but Black's king is badly placed. The latter factor is of

Capablanca-Tartakover
142   New York 1924

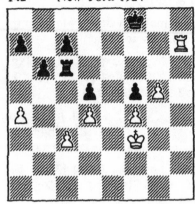

great importance here, and if White can bring his king into the attack as well, then owing to the passed g-pawn Black's position may become critical.

Therefore, White played **1 ♔g3!! ♖xc3+ 2 ♔h4 ♖f3 3 g6! ♖xf4+ 4 ♔g5 ♖e4 5 ♔f6!**

The king's bishop's pawn will not run off anywhere. It is much more important for White to create threats against the black king at once.

5 ... ♔g8 6 ♖g7+ ♔h8 7 ♖xc7 ♖e8 8 ♔xf5 ♖e4 9 ♔f6 ♖f4+ 10 ♔e5 ♖g4 11 g7+ ♔g8 12 ♖xa7 ♖g1 13 ♔xd5 ♖c1 14 ♔d6 ♖c2 15 d5 ♖c1 16 ♖c7 ♖a1 17 ♔c6 ♖xa4 18 d6, and **Black resigned**.

This example shows yet again that in rook endings the active placing of the pieces usually redeems sacrificed material with interest.

Queen Endings

During our examination of the ending of queen and pawn against queen we discovered that in certain cases the stronger side's queen could overcome the resistance of the opponent's queen and promote the pawn single-handed, without the assistance of the king. This possibility is of very special importance in endings in which both sides have pawns.

143

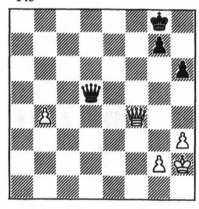

Thus, in the above position, the white king is securely defended against checks. By continuing **1 ♕b8+ ♔f7 2 b5**, White easily exploits his passed pawn extra. For example:

2 ... ♔e7

Black tries to bring his king across to help.

3 ♕c7+ ♔e6 4 b6 ♕d6+

White threatened 5 b7, queening the pawn.

5 ♕xd6+ ♔xd6 6 ♔g3 ♔c6 7 ♔f4 ♔xb6 8 ♔f5 ♔c5 9 ♔g6, and White wins.

This example was ideal, of course. The white pieces co-operated with each other smoothly and the queen, in particular, performed great work. It supported the advance of the passed pawn and covered the king at the same time.

Exploiting an extra pawn in a queen ending is not usually an easy matter. The slightest pawn weakness in the cover around the stronger side's king may allow the opponent to threaten perpetual check and so render it difficult to realise the material advantage. It is especially important to remember here that sometimes, when the king is unable to find shelter in its own camp, a bold advance with it into the enemy position may prove a more effective means of escape.

Thus, if the stronger side's king is unable to hide from the checks behind its own pawns, it is obliged to venture out into the 'open sea' and there seek a defence against perpetual check. The following two examples show how in this case it is possible to hide from the pursuit of the opponent's queen.

Maroczy-Bogoljubow
144   Dresden 1936   **W**

White cannot win a pawn by 1 ♕xc6, since after 1 ... ♕f4+ 2 ♔g1 ♕c1+ Black gives perpetual check. He wins by sacrificing a pawn, with the aim of creating a passed pawn.

1 b5! cxb5 2 c6 ♕c2 3 ♕d5

3 c7 was simpler.

3 ... ♔h6 4 ♕d6 ♕c4 5 c7 ♔h7 6 ♕d7!

It is impossible to promote the pawn here without the help of the king, so White stops preventing the queen checks, and sends his king off on a lengthy journey, the terminal point of which is b7.

6 ... ♕f4+ 7 ♔g1 ♕c1+ 8 ♔f2 ♕c5+ 9 ♔e2 ♕c2+ 10 ♔e3 ♕c5+ 11 ♔e4 ♕c4+ 12 ♔e5 ♕c3+ 13 ♔d5 ♕c4+ 14 ♔d6 ♕b4+ 15 ♔c6 ♕c3+ 16 ♔b7

White has achieved his aim, and the pawn cannot be stopped.

As will be seen, the black b-pawn became an excellent screen for White's king. Therefore he was correct to avoid capturing it on the 4th move.

In the above example the king found shelter in the opponent's camp, where it was defended from checks along the file by an enemy pawn. Here is another, no less important, way of hiding from checks.

Maroczy-Betbeder
145   Hamburg 1930   **B**

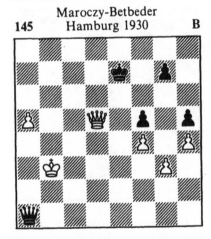

A rook's pawn is poorer than all other pawns in helping a king to hide from checks. But here White succeeds in avoiding the pursuit by exploiting the position of the opponent's king. This procedure, which we met earlier in the ending of queen and pawn against queen, is very important in any type of queen ending.

1 ... ♛b1+ 2 ♚a4 g6 3 a6 ♛a1+ 4 ♚b5 ♛b2+ 5 ♚c6 ♛f6+ 6 ♚c7!

Note this move. If now 6 ... ♛xa6, then 7 ♛d7+ and 8 ♛d6+, exchanging queens and transposing into a won pawn ending.

6 ... ♛c3+ 7 ♛c6 ♛e3 8 ♚c8!

Black resigned: 8 ... ♚f7 is met by 9 a7! ♛xa7 10 ♛d7+, exchanging queens with an easy win. Thanks to the poor position of the opponent's king, White's task was not at all difficult.

In the general run of such endings the centralised position of the queen usually guarantees the king's escape from persecution. However, in moving the king about the board, one should always remember that in conjunction with pawns a queen can easily construct a mating net around the king. Consider the position in diagram 146.

White will win if he can break free with his king and go over to the c-pawn. Therefore, in answer to 1 ... ♛f1+ he played 2 ♚g4, intending to bring the king out. Against 2 ... ♛f5+ 3 ♚h4 ♛f3 he proposed, evidently, to play 4 ♛d8+ ♚g7 5 ♛f6+!, transposing into a won pawn ending. But White's second move unexpectedly turned out to be a terrible mistake. Black replied 2 ... f5+!, and it became clear that whatever White

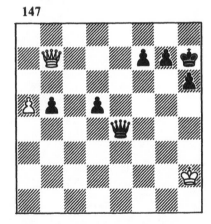

played, mate was unavoidable. For example, **3 gxf6 ♛f5+ 4 ♚h4 ♛h5 mate** or **3 ♚h4 ♛h1 mate**. A tragi-comic finale!

147

Even when one side has a big material superiority, the presence of just one enemy passed pawn may balance the chances.

Thus, although Black has four

(!!) extra pawns in this position, he is hardly likely to achieve more than perpetual check after White's **1 a6**.

Printed in the USA
CPSIA information can be obtained
at www.ICGtesting.com
JSHW021913100224
57071JS00001B/8